# Travellers' Tales

of

# Sandwich

compiled by

# T. L. Richardson

© Published by the Sandwich Local History Society,
May, 2002

ISBN: 0-9542424-1-6

# Preface

The primary aim of this study, which is based upon a wide range of contemporary literary accounts, is to provide a series of insights into the history of Sandwich and its people since the mid fifteenth century. About one hundred rare books, obscure articles and out-of-print journals were consulted and the diverse views and opinions found in these publications have been collated in chronological order to form the main body of the text. Given certain unavoidable gaps and imbalances in the evidence, the reader will find that many of the following impressions and descriptions of Sandwich were not only conditioned by various deep-seated preferences and prejudices, but they were also strongly influenced by an acute awareness of the many misfortunes and disasters of the town's past. Indeed, a veritable spectrum of differing moods and perspectives, ranging from the pessimistic to the optimistic, are represented in the text. Hence, we find that Sandwich is depicted in times of stagnation and depression, when unemployment and social misery were widespread in the town, as well as in times of expansion and growth, when rising incomes and material wealth were in evidence for all to see. Not only does this compilation provide a series of graphic insights into many aspects of the town and its community over a very long period of time, but it also says much about the various forces which influenced the overall pace and direction of its development at various stages in its history.

This study owes a sizeable debt of gratitude to a number of institutions and individuals. In particular, I would like to thank the Sandwich Local History Society for funding this publication, and Dr. Frank Andrews, whose expertise and enthusiasm were largely responsible for bringing this work to completion. I would also like to acknowledge the help of Mrs. Jo-Ann Buck, for reading the text and correcting my errors, and Mr.E.J. Sidery for permitting me to draw upon the W.H. Boyer collection of photographs, and Mr. Charles Wanostrocht for providing a number of the illustrations. I am also grateful to the librarians of the British Library, the University of Kent, the Sandwich Local History Archive and the Deal, Canterbury and Sandwich public libraries for providing all the literary material used in this study.

# Introduction

> Of all the glee undire Gode so glade ware they neuere
> As of the sounde of the see and Sandwyche belles

The diaries, journals and memoirs of the many travellers who visited Sandwich over the past five hundred years constitutes a valuable source of historical evidence. The various descriptions and impressions of Sandwich recorded by these people not only throw considerable light upon the nature of contemporary social attitudes and values, but they also provide us with a rare and fascinating glimpse of the town and its community at various points in time.

In view of the town's isolated position on the Channel coast, and the poor condition of the East Kent roads, very few travellers were able to visit Sandwich during the Middle Ages. Indeed, the main route to Sandwich during this period was via the sea, and most of its visitors tended to be either foreign merchants or military expeditionary forces going abroad. Nevertheless, the literary accounts left by these visitors are important in that they provide us with a unique insight into the early character of the town and its riparian community. From these records we learn, for example, that as a result of Sandwich's proximity to the English Channel, and the ever-present threat posed by marauding buccaneers and hostile French warships, it was necessary to defend the town with a series of ditches, earthen ramparts, stone walls and gateways at the points where it 'stondeth most in jeopardi of ennemies.' Similarly, a Bohemian nobleman, who saw 'fleets' of Venetian and Genoese cogs, galleys and carracks at anchor in Sandwich haven in 1446, provides a rare glimpse of the type, size and origin of the vessels trading through its port. Natural disasters, involving the loss of life and the destruction of property, were avidly recorded, as was the most catastrophic event in the town's history - the silting-up of its harbour by an unstoppable tide of water-borne sand, silt and mud. Periodic visits by the great and the good, and the townsfolk's response to these occasions, were also described in some detail. The Archbishop of Canterbury's visit one 'foul and rainy' day in 1563 was duly recorded, as was the somewhat grander visit of Elizabeth I in 1573 when 'all the Towne was graveled and strewed with rushes, herbs, flags, and suche lyke.'

During the later seventeenth and eighteenth centuries, as increasing numbers of travellers found their way to the town, a more complete picture of Sandwich begins to emerge. Indeed, the remarkable increase in geographical mobility during this period took place largely as a result of two socio-economic developments: the systematic building of a network of turnpike roads throughout the south-eastern region, and a growing willingness to embark upon long tours of discovery around the English countryside. The newly built toll-roads not only opened up the remoter parts of the kingdom to travellers, but they also stimulated an enthusiasm for the delights and wonders of the wider world: Arcadian landscapes, picturesque seascapes, historic towns and ancient ruins. The discovery of hidden delights such as these stirred the travellers' imaginations, aroused their emotions and helped to satisfy their innate curiosity. In responding to the widening opportunities before them, increasing numbers of educated middle-class people of independent means, braving the dangers and discomforts of inclement weather, squalid wayside inns and predatory highwaymen, set out with their maps and guide books upon long and arduous journeys around East Kent. At first by horseback, stage-coach and carriage, and later on by steam train and motor car, an impressive number of talented individuals from many walks of life - political commentators, economists, popular journalists, antiquarian historians, county topographers, agronomists, travel writers, famous diarists, artists, poets, picturesque tourists and their kind - began to find their way to the outer reaches of East Kent and so to the ancient town and port of Sandwich. Foremost amongst these travellers were Celia Fiennes (1642 - 1741), the 'sober, matter-of-fact, plain-spoken' daughter of a Cromwellian colonel; John Evelyn (1620-1706), the Restoration diarist; Daniel Defoe (1661-1731), the author of *Robinson Crusoe* and the 'father of modem journalism'; Arthur Young (1741-1820), the 'apostle of the Agricultural Revolution'; and William Cobbett (1762-1835), 'England's greatest radical' and 'Quixotic defender' of the common man. Other notable visitors to the town included Edward Hasted (1732- 1812),the antiquarian author of one of the 'finest of the great Hanoverian county histories of England'; Elizabeth Carter (1717-1806), the poet, translator and literary associate of Dr. Samuel Johnson; and John Wesley (1703-1791), the founder of Methodism in England.

It is evident from the contemporary literary accounts assembled here that all these individuals were acute observers of the world through which they passed. Very little escaped their eyes and, being highly articulate and opinionated, they suffered no inhibitions in expressing their thoughts about the town and its community; especially the condition of the Stour, the state of agriculture, industry and trade, the atmosphere of the town and the unique character of its architecture. Views on what they liked and disliked about Sandwich were expressed with arguable weights of emphasis and objectivity, and these ranged from the acerbic to the poetic. Celia Fiennes, Daniel Defoe and William Cobbett, for example, variously described Sandwich as a 'sad', 'old decay'd, poor, miserable' town, and 'as villainous a hole as one could wish to see', whilst those in a more appreciative frame of mind were attracted by the 'quiet beauty' and 'picturesque interior' of the 'pretty and well built' town: a 'clean,' 'neat', 'quaint', 'old-fashioned' town with 'many fair streets' and a 'cleare' fresh-water stream (the Delf) 'about knee deepe' flowing through it. Idiosyncratic impressions such as these varied from visitor to visitor, as well as from time to time, and were strongly influenced by an awareness of the various forces which had conspired to shape its destiny. The silting of the town's deep- water anchorage during the later Middle Ages, and the subsequent falling-away of its once substantial overseas trade with France, Italy and the Low Countries, had a profound and lasting influence upon contemporary attitudes towards Sandwich; as indeed did the Dutch-inspired textile and horticultural boom of the later sixteenth century, the succession of industrial and demographic crises of the seventeenth century and the alternating periods of economic expansion, contraction and stagnation during the eighteenth and nineteenth centuries. Long-term trends and developments of this sort not only led to a marked reduction in the level of industrial and commercial activity in Sandwich, but they also, in the absence of any newly emerging dynamic forces of economic change, tended to preserve, rather than transform, the town's old-world character.

The sights and sounds of Sandwich, when seen and heard from afar, had a captivating influence upon most travellers. For these, the 'incredible clangour' of 'sweet bells', which Cobbett once heard some two miles away as he rode along a 'beautiful road' from Deal to Sandwich, and the gradual appearance of the town's Caen stone and cupola- topped church towers and red pantiled rooftops above the low East Kent horizon, were the earliest signs that their destination was near. One traveller, approaching the town from the north, noted that 'the wind blows keenly across the stretches of desolate marsh-lands, clouds sail overhead, their shadows coursing across the green sward', whilst another thought that the town looked its best at sunset when it gradually sank 'into the shadows of the night ... becoming more indistinct as the shadows lengthened and night followed hard upon declining day'. Indeed, the town, when seen at a distance in a flattering light, when 'slanting rays of mellowed sunshine pour through towering clouds, when rain impends and the dun of the marshes takes on a fresher green', only served to draw the approaching traveller on and into its timeless embrace. The fact that the town occupied a low position within the coastal marshlands only served to emphasise the vast expanse of sky all around it:

> From horizon to horizon there is no single elevation to cast a shadow or to intercept the sunshine. Only when clouds are riding and sea winds sweeping over, are the bright colours of the town and its gleaming belt of meadow and river obscured.

Looking outwards from the town into the East Kent countryside, from the top of St. Clement's church tower, another glorious panoramic view was to be had:

> Afar, on a clear day, the view includes Reculver; and when the low fog hangs over the marshes, the insularity of Thanet is unmistakable. From the back of Ash the chalk hills bound the view round to the South Foreland, and from there the gleam of the coast of France dies out in the wide expanse of the sea.

The area around Sandwich, according to Cobbett and others, contained 'some of the finest land in the world'; cornfields, market gardens, orchards and rich meadows. As one seventeenth century traveller put it, a 'Paradice of pleasant Meads and fertile Marishes, fruitfull and delightfull Fields of Corne'. Visitors who approached the town from the west, via the Roman road which linked Canterbury to Richborough Castle, passed through an area that was so productive of wheat, barley, hops and orchard fruits that John Evelyn described it as a 'sweete garden'; a garden which 'infinitely delighted' him because it was 'the best cultivated of any that in my life I had anywhere seene.'. Similarly, those who rode towards Sandwich from the south or the east passed through one of the most fertile market-gardening areas in the kingdom; an area that was renowned in London's vegetable markets for the excellence of its carrots, lettuce, radishes, artichokes, asparagus, peas and beans. Travellers who approached the town from the north, on the other hand, via the road which crossed the former bed of the Wantsum Channel, passed through a much harsher landscape; a landscape that was characterised by 'flagged marshes', 'fields of long tasselled reed grass' and 'meadow-lands covered with sheep ... dykes and watercourses'. Not only did 'bleak' north-easterly winds blow with a 'singular rigidity' across these lonely marsh-lands, but it was also an area where the traveller encountered the river Stour, a 'leisurely piece of water bordered by bands of rushes and meadow-sweet'; a 'sluggishly serpentine' river which followed a 'meandering', 'winding', 'curving', 'sinuous' course to the distant 'faithless' sea. Whilst some described the town's ancient link with the outside world as a 'shrunken stream ... in a heavy bed if still accumulating sand', others saw the river and its setting in a more poetic light:

> How the horizon arches overhead
> Its stainless sapphire, and the river glides
> With plaintive murmurs o'er its sandy bed
> To mingle with the foam of Ocean's tides.

Many other interesting features attracted the attention of the approaching traveller; especially the 'sprinkling' of windmills around the town, the salt water evaporation pits along the Thanet road, the rust red sails of barges, colliers and hoys moving up and down the Stour, and the 'towering, mossy, frowning' walls of Richborough Castle - 'To whose grey walls the sunless ivy clings ...The roofless halls of conquerors and kings'. Other aspects of interest to the picturesque tourist included the 'grass edged open road', the lines of poplar trees that 'quivered in the dancing reflection' of the watercourses, the 'endless distances of the unbroken marshes', the 'garden spaces' and 'drying fields', the sheep pastures and meadows where 'sportive heifers court the noontide ray'. To many visitors, this composite picture, when set against the town's 'crenellated red roofs ... picked out with tile shadows', tended to give Sandwich a distinctive 'Dutch look'. As one such visitor said, 'the quaint, foreign-looking aspect of the place never fails to strike ...[one] with surprise', whilst others thought that it resembled an 'old Flemish picture', and declared that 'one must go to Holland to find anything to surpass it'. Sandwich, therefore, appeared to be 'almost more Dutch or Flemish than English'; in fact, a typical 'Low Country seventeenth-century town' such as 'Bruges made smaller, sweeter and more radiant'.

On entering Sandwich, most visitors were immediately struck by its 'strangely old-world Plantagenet character'. 'You seem to breathe an atmosphere connected directly with the past', noted one enthusiast, 'an atmosphere of long ago that will not leave it', while another thought that the town was permeated with a 'flavour of death and dust'. 'You almost expect to scent the fustiness of an unwashed town' noted another visitor, 'that musty air that issues from unventilated attics and dark, disused passages'. Perhaps that is why Fussell, after visiting Sandwich in 1818 likened his experience to 'the solemn sadness of a visit to Herculaneum or Pompeia', Indeed, many visitors who were familiar with the silting-up of the town's deep-water anchorage, and the subsequent falling away of its overseas trade, wrote in a similar vein. Hence, Sandwich was frequently depicted as a 'deserted' town, left 'high and dry' by the retreating sea; a 'drowsy', 'motionless', 'sleepy' town whose 'half-deserted' streets 'dreaded the turf's encroaching green'.

In view of the town's imperceptible advance towards modernity, these observations were broadly true. As some of its critics pointed out, Sandwich appeared to suffer from a 'dearth of public spirit' as well as a 'drowsy stupid contentment with things as they are'. As far as the town's economic health was concerned, not only did it suffer from a static internal market, due to a negligible rate of population increase, but it also possessed few industries. Most of these were traditional, small-scale, low-wage, labour-intensive, craft-based industries such as shipbuilding, tanning, brewing and malting; industries whose *raison d'être* was to serve the demands and needs of the local community rather than those of the wider market economy. Hence, the bulk of the commodities entering into the town's water-borne trade tended to be derived from its rural hinterland. These consisted, in the main, of wheat, barley, hops, malt, apples, pears, cherries and vegetables, and most of these were shipped to London and various other east coast ports. Most of the goods brought into the town consisted of coal, iron, timber, groceries and 'shop goods', and these were mainly obtained from London, Norway, Sweden and other Baltic states.

The architectural fabric of Sandwich had a considerable impact upon its visitors; especially its medieval stone and flint walls, gateways, earthen ramparts and ditches; a parallelogram shaped structure some 'five furlongs in length from east to west, and two and a half from north to south.' Contained within this 'oblong square', and to the delight of antiquarian historians and picturesque tourists alike, lay a wealth of ancient churches, almshouses and hospitals, as well as a grammar school, guildhall, barbican and toll-bridge. Indeed, an eclectic range of buildings that were constructed from a variety of local and imported materials of differing texture and colour: dark oak beams, Flemish bricks, Kentish ragstone, Caen stone, Dutch pantiles, Kent peg tiles and knapped flint. As most visitors were to avow, a rich assembly of primary materials which defined the architectural character of the town and contributed much to its picturesque quality.

Until the mid eighteenth century, when a small number of well-to-do dwellings in High Street, Fisher Street and Delf Street were re-faced in brick and given fashionable sliding sash windows, elegant Georgian door-cases and fanlights in the London mode, the majority of the domestic dwellings in Sandwich were timber framed.

> Nearly all the houses in all the streets are old. Early Georgian ... is the prevailing type ... though who is to say how many ancient structures lurk behind a Georgian front! [for] among these mellow brick fronts there are still to be seen unaltered great numbers of half-timbered Tudor and Jacobean buildings, many with projecting upper storeys.

A wide range of opinions were expressed on the aesthetic value of these buildings. Whilst some described the houses in the 'somewhat squalid streets' as 'dirty, inconvenient little places', or 'old-fashioned', 'ill-built', 'primitive', 'rude, mean and low', many others, after perambulating some of the better-off streets, expressed their admiration for 'staid and substantial old houses ... mellowed and blackened with age'; houses whose windows and 'chance-opened doors' revealed comfort and prosperity within and 'glimpses of old-fashioned gardens and orchards ... and verdant patches of lawn, leaf and blossom'. As one visitor put it,

> ... nearly all the houses are little ... [their] gardens have trellised gates, affording glimpses of garden mysteries beyond. Their fruit trees ... take the lines of those one sees in the gardens of foreign inns; children peep through the gate-bars as if through convent grilles ... through the doorways one sees windows beyond, little square windows with muslin curtains.

The rich legacy of ancient buildings in Sandwich was, as many visitors were to confirm, fully complemented by an 'intricate jumble' of winding, twisting streets. These streets, which were laid-out in medieval times, were frequently the cause of some frustration (as well as delight) and were variously described as 'ill-convenient lanes, little adapted either for carriages or even horses'; a 'tortuous maze' of cobbled streets 'broken into many disagreeable angles'. When Lady Mary Coke passed through the town in 1788 she complained that the streets were so narrow that 'there is not room for two carriages to pass', while another visitor, writing in 1837, declared that the streets were 'actually dangerous for a carriage to travel through' owing to 'lumps of mortar, bricks and other rubbish lying for nights together'. Such was the 'crooked', 'irregular' and 'deceptive' nature of the streets that the general belief was that 'If they strike other streets ... at any angle it seems to be rather by accident than design', whilst others thought that the town had deliberately designed its streets in the form of a maze in order to 'keep you inside for all time'. 'You are continually missing the point at which you aim', noted one baffled visitor, 'continually passing the same spot', whilst another commented ,'you are almost certain, while endeavouring to reach a particular point within the town, to find yourself brought up short on the ramparts, in the open country, or by the river, or quite possibly at the very spot from whence you started!' Other visitors echoed these sentiments:

> The only complaint that the average visitor makes is that although it may be easy to get into the town it's very difficult to find his way out. He traverses a street which apparently takes him to the Canterbury road but its odds against him reaching his desired goal. He twists and turns and finds himself back in the place from whence he started. He makes another attempt - with the same result. He has lost his bearings utterly ...

The 'mysterious courts and alley-ways' that led from these streets, like the many 'passages that led to nothing', constituted an important part of the town's unique character - as indeed did many other outstanding features such as the arcaded Caen stone Norman tower of St. Clement's parish church, the lead ogee cupola - 'a kind of Dutch bulb' - of St. Peter's parish church, the medieval two-storeyed flint and stone Fisher Gate, the black and white chequered twin towers of the Barbican - 'the most fitting entrance to the town for a visitor' - and the Delf Stream:

> One of the peculiarities of this ... town is the water-supply ... Sandwich rejoices in a freshwater river that runs in and out of the old streets ... clear, fresh, and two or three feet in depth ... by doorways and under bow-windows ... to supply a pump, or to answer the claims of buckets, brought down flights of steps connected with ancient houses. Then it will slip away under some old tunnel, to dash out again by green lawns and gardens, and to reappear in the quiet streets.

Most visitors to Sandwich commented on the day-to-day sounds of the town: the intermittent rattle of cranes and winches on the quays and wharves, the clatter of carts and wagons in the cobble-stoned streets, the noise of bullocks, sheep and pigs being driven on the hoof to the market place, and the 'confused sweet jumble' of church bells ringing out across the rooftops - 'chiming the quarters and striking the hours, and the whole eight of them pealing for services and weddings and rejoicings and practisings, and the tenor going every morning at five as the rising bell and at eight o'clock every evening as the curfew bell'. Indeed, the everyday sights and sounds of Sandwich conspired to give it an ambience that few visitors could resist. The fact that very little changed in Sandwich over the course of time, whilst the world at large moved on, only served to enhance its allure to the enchanted traveller.

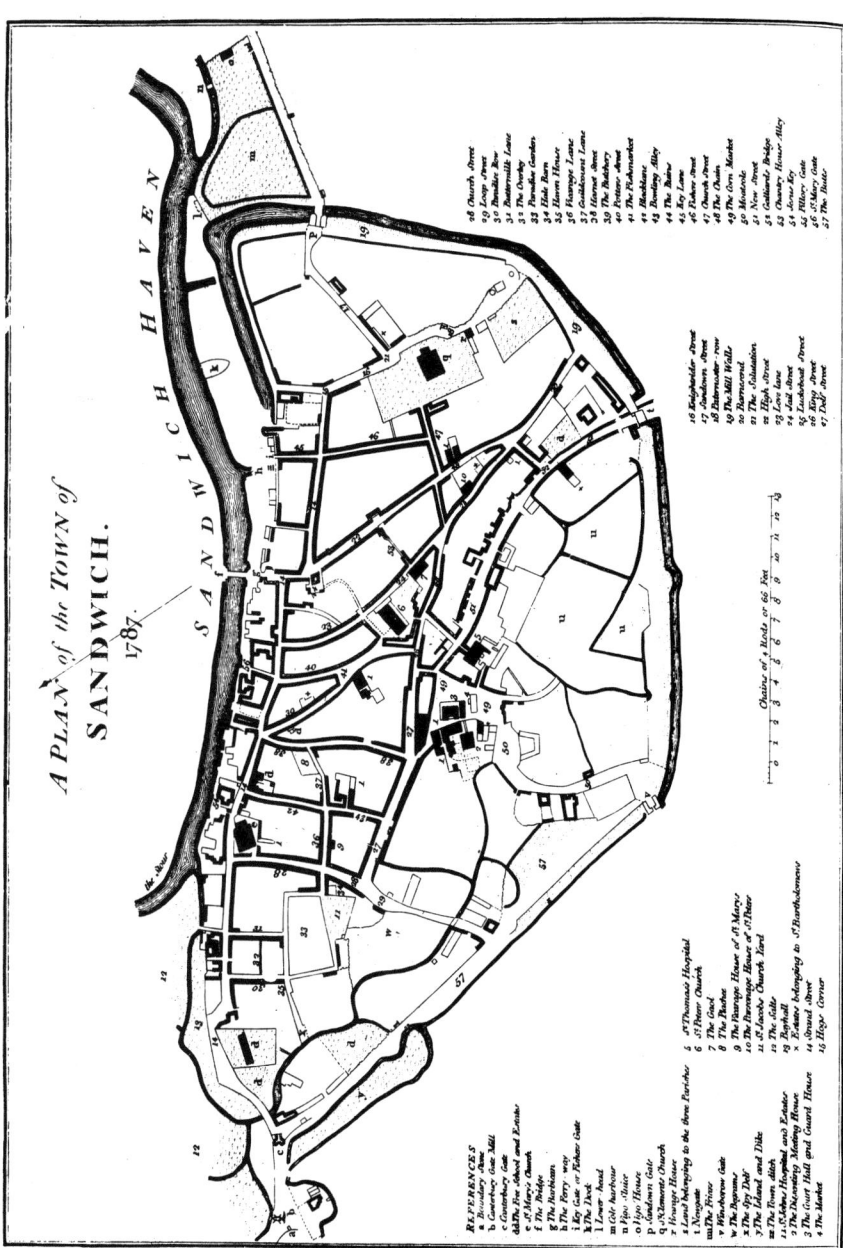

Taken from Boys' 'History'

# Travellers' Tales

**Medieval Sandwich.**

Because of the town's favourable position on the Channel coast, mid-way between London and the French coast, Sandwich was able to play an important role in the waging of the Hundred Years' War (1337-1453). Indeed, the intermittent bouts of warfare arising out of England's claim to the French crown and the sovereignty of Gascony made heavy demands upon the ships and men of the Cinque Ports. As a designated rendezvous point for the King's navy and military expeditionary forces going abroad, many thousands of men-at-arms and their equipment (siege-engines, weapons, provisions and horses) were assembled at Sandwich in readiness for the short sea-crossing to England's military garrison at Calais or the battlefields of Normandy, Brittany and Gascony. Despite the dangers posed to merchantmen by Breton pirates and enemy warships in the English Channel and the Bay of Biscay, and the firing and sacking of Sandwich by a large French military force in 1457, the town managed to sustain a vibrant two-way trade with some of the most economically advanced towns and regions in Western Europe. Large amounts of Kentish wool were exported through Sandwich to Calais, where it was bought by Flemish clothiers, whilst substantial quantities of industrial raw materials, luxury goods and utilitarian wares were shipped into the town by Dutch and Spanish vessels, as well as by some of the most celebrated trading fleets in medieval Europe, especially the Venetians, Genoese and Florentines. Until the later fifteenth century, when the town's deep-water anchorage began to silt up, this trade enabled Sandwich to enjoy a period of unprecedented wealth and prosperity. At that juncture the town had a population of "good and able mariners belonging to the navy of it ... above the number of 1500" and between 800 and 900 buildings: wealthy merchant houses, a Carmelite priory, three fine parish churches and a numbers of almshouses and hospitals for the sick and needy. In view of the many hit-and-run attacks that were taking place along the south coast during this period, all these buildings were enclosed within a defensive ring of stone walls, gateways, earthen ramparts and ditches.

**1446** On the third day ... we held our course towards England. And as we were approaching, we beheld lofty heights full of chalk ... Passing by those heights ... we approached the town of Sandwich; this lies near the sea, so that many regions can be visited in ships therefrom. This is the first of the towns of England to be met with on that coast. Here I first beheld fleets of vessels, ships, galleons, and cogs. That is called a ship, which is driven by the winds alone. That is a galleon, which is propelled by oars: some of them have more than two hundred rowers. This kind of vessel is of great size and length, by which means it can be navigated both in favourable and in adverse winds. With it, for the most part, maritime wars have been accustomed to be waged, especially as it can hold some hundreds of men at the same time. The third kind is that which they call a cog, and is tolerably large. But nothing did I admire more than the sailors climbing the mast, and foretelling the approach of the winds and their distance, and giving instructions what sails were to be hoisted, and which to be lowered. Among them I saw one sailor so agile, that scarcely can any one be compared with him. There is a custom at Sandwich that [men] walk about all night with trumpets and other musical instruments, calling out and announcing what wind is blowing at that time. On hearing this, if a wind is reported to be blowing convenient for them, they [the mariners] sally forth, board their ships, and direct their course towards their own countries (Baron L. von Rozmital). [1]

**1457** This yere ... the Sencyall of Normandy, Sir Peers the Brasyle, and Flokket, came with iijM men and londyd be syde Sandwyche, and toke the towne and spoyled hit, and toke a way myche goode, and slewe dyverse persones, and toke many prisoners: but the contre came downe and drove hem a wey, and in her fleynge to shippe ther were drowned mo than vj$^{xx}$ men of the Frensshe parties (Anon).[2]

**1457** A nauye or flote of Frenshemen landyd at Sandwyche, & spoylyd & robbed the towne, and exercysed there great crueltie ... syr Piers de Bresy, seneshall of Normandy, with the capytayne of Depe, and many other capytayns of Fraunce, came with a great and stronge nauy into the Downys by nyght, and vpon the morrowe came certeyne of them vnto Sandewyche, & there spoyled and robbyd the towne, and toke with them great prayes and many ryche prysoners ...( R. Fabyan).[3]

**1520** Sandwich ....is two leagues from Dover in the English Downs as you go towards Zealand. Great vessels cannot come alongside there, but may anchor two leagues off, at the turn of the Downs, without danger from any tempest, except one of extraordinary violence, and with a favourable wind they can cross in three hours to Flanders. Small or middle sized ships can come to the wall of the town, which is about as large as Vilvorde, but better built, and with houses more suitable for lodging men without horses .... still it is the nearest port to Flanders, and therefore more convenient than Southampton (Bishop of Elna and Jehan de la Sauch).[4]

**1520** The town of Sandwich is only a small and poor place, devoid of any houses in which the King of England could receive the King of the Romans in a befitting manner(Anon).[5]

**1535-1543** Sandwic, on the farther side of the ryver of Sture, is meatly welle walled wher the town stondeth most in jeopardi of ennemies. The residew

13

of the town is dichid and mudde waulled. Ther be yn the town iiii. principal gates, iii. paroche chyrches, of the which sum suppose that St. Marye's was sumtyme a nunnery. Ther is a place of Whit freres, and an hospital withowt the town fyrst ordened for maryners desesid and hurt. Ther is a place wher the monkes of Christ Chirch did resort when they were lordes of the towne. The caryke that was sonke yn the haven yn Pope Paulus tyme did much hurt to the haven, and gether a great banke. The grounde self from Sandwiche to the haven, and inward to the land is caullid Sanded Bay... though now Sandwich be not celebrated by cawse of Goodwine Sandes, and the decay of the haven (J. Leland).[6]

**1552-3** In this yere the sea broke in at Sandwitch, in so moche that it did overflow all the marshes there about, and drouned moch cattail, to the great losse bothe of the toune and the countrey (R.Fabyan).[7]

## Elizabethan and Carolean Sandwich.

The early modern history of Sandwich was profoundly affected by a number of important events; the arrival of a sizeable number of Protestant refugees from the Spanish Netherlands during the 1560s, and the waging of an acrimonious trade war between England and Holland during the later seventeenth century. Although the introduction of market-garden crops (peas, carrots, radishes and parsnips) and new and improved methods of cloth making into Sandwich by Dutch and Walloon farmer-craftsmen helped to offset the loss of its haven and revitalise its flagging economy, the town's North Sea trade was periodically disrupted by the Anglo-Dutch conflict. Continental markets were temporarily closed and merchants, fearing an attack by Dutch warships, preferred to keep their vessels in port. A series of outbreaks of the plague during this period only served to deepen the crisis. High and rising mortality rates far exceeded the number of baptisms in Sandwich, and the population therefore began to fall. This loss was further worsened by an exodus of skilled workers to other towns. Indeed, the only redeeming development during these difficult years was the growth of the town's coasting trade in agricultural produce with London and the rapidly growing dockyard towns and ports of north-west Kent.

**1563** ... our pious Archbishop ... rode on Sunday morning from his house at Bekesborn to Sandwich, which was about five or six miles; and got thither by seven o'clock; that by coming so soon he might prevent their formalities of receiving him, and partly to be present at their whole service. But notwithstanding, the townsmen prevented him: for though that morning were very foul and rainy, yet he found the Mayor and his Jurats ready at the town gate to accompany him to his lodging, and so to the church. Of whom he gave this character to a friend at Court, 'That they were men of honest civility, and of comely grave personages, and of good understanding. And that their streets were clean, as might be for the straitness of them. That their service was sung in good distinct harmony and quiet devotion. That the singing men were the Mayor and the Jurats, with the head men of the town, placed in the quire far and distant, in as good order as he could wish.' The Archbishop himself then preached before an auditory great and attentive ... And, in sum, to their credit he said of them, 'That he saw not, but the Queen's Majesty would have of them good subjects and true orators.'

Thus being here according to his function, he inquired diligently into the behaviour of the inhabitants, as likewise of the strangers, who had fled hither for the sake of the Gospel from foreign parts, whether French or Dutch ... and had here settled themselves. Of these also he took notice and found them ... very godly on the Sabbath day, and busy in their work on the week day: and their quietness such, as the Mayor and his brethren had no causes of variance between themselves, coming before them ... 'Profitable and gentle strangers (they are his own words) ought to be welcome, and not to be grudged at' (J. Strype).[8]

1570    This Towne ... came to ruine by the alteration and vicissitude of the Sea, which peradventure choked the haven thereof with light sand ... cheefly by the abundance of the light sand ... it is declined to great decay ... (W. Lambarde).[9]

1573    The queen arrives at Sandwich on monday 31st august about seven in the evening; 'at whiche tyme John Gylbart, maior, accompanied with ix jurats, the townclarke and some of the comen counsell receaved her highnes at Sandowne at the uttermost ende thereof, the said maior beinge appareled in a scarlet gowne, at which place her maiestie stayed. And there the said maior yelden up to her maiestie his mace. And not far from them stoode thre hundreth persons or thereabowts apparalled in whyte doblets with blacke and whyt rybon in the sleves, black gascoyne hose and whyte garters, euery of them having a muryon and a calyver or di. musket, having thre dromes and thre ensignes and thre capitans, *viz.* mr Alexander Cobbe, mr Edward Peake, and mr Edward Wood, jurats; euery of theis dischardged their shott, her maiesty being at downes gate. And duringe her maiesties standinge and receavinge of the mace the great ordynance was dischardged, which was to the number of one hundreth or cxx; and that in such good order as the quene and noble men gave great comendacion thereof, and sayd, that Sandwich should have the honor aswell for the good order thereof as also of their small shott.

Then her maiestie went towards the town, and at Sandowne gate were a lyon and a dragon, all gilt set up uppon ii posts at the bridge ende, and her armes was hanged up uppon the gate. All the towne was graveled and strewed with rushes, herbs, flags and suche lyke, euery howse havinge a nomber of grene bowes standing against the dores and walls, every howse paynted whyte and black. Her maiestie rode into the towne, and in dyvers places as far as her lodginge were dyvers cords made of vine branches with their leaves hanking crosse the streats; and uppon them dyvers garlands of fyne flowers. And so she rode forth till she came directly over against mr Cripps howses almost as far as the pellicane, where stood a fyne howse newly buylt and vaulted, over wheron her armes was sett and hanked with tapestrye. In the same stode Rychard Spycer minister of st Clements parishe, a mr. of art, the townes orator, apparrelled in a blacke gown and a hoode both lyned and faced with black taffatye being the guyfte of the towne, accompanied with the other ii ministers and the schole master. He made unto her highnes an oration ... which she so well lyked as she gaue thereof a singuler comendacion, sayenge it was both very well handeled and very elloquent. Then he presented her with a cupp of gold of a Cl. which Thomas Gylbart sonne to the maior aforesaid receaved from mr Spycer, and he gave yt to the footemen; of whome her maiestie receaved yt, and so delyvered yt to mr Rauffe Lane one of the gent. equirries, who caried yt. And then the said mr Spycer presented her with a new testament in greeke, which she thankefully accepted. And so rode untill she came unto mr Manwood's howse, wherin she lodged, a howse wherein kinge Henry the viiith had ben lodged twyes before. And here is to be noted that uppon euery post and corner from her first entrye to her lodginge wer fixed certen verses, and against the court gate all thoes verses put into a table and there hanged up.

The nexte daye beinge twysdaye and the first of september, the towne havinge buylded a forte at Stoner on thother syde of the havon, the capitanes aforesaid led over their men to assault the said forte; during which tyme certen wallounds that could well swym had prepared two boats, and in thende of eche boate a borde uppon which bords stode a man, and so met together with either of them a staffe and a sheld of woodd, and one of them did over throwe an other; at which the quene had good sport. And that don the capitans put their men into a battayle, and takeng with them some lose shott gave the scarmerche to the forte, and in the ende, after the dischardge of ii fawkenets and certen chambers, after dyvers assaults the forte was wonne.

The next daye, viz. wednesdaye the second of september, mrs mayres and her sisters the jurats wyves made the quenes majestie a banket of clx disshes on a table of xxviii foote long in the scole howse; and so her majestie came thether thorough mrs Manwoods garden and thoroughe mr Woods also, the ways beinge hanked with black and whyte bayes; and in the scole howse garden mr Isebrand made unto her an oration, and presented to her highnes a cupp of silver and guylt with a cover to the same well nere a cubit highe, to whome her majestie answered this, "Gaudeo me in hoc natum esse ut vobis et ecclesie Dei prosim" and so entered into the scole howse, wheare she was very merrye and did eate of dyvers disshes withowt any assaye, and caused certen to be reserved for her and carried to her lodginge.

The next daye, being thursdaye and the daye of her departinge, against the scole howse upon the new turfed wall and uppon a scaffold made uppon the wall of the scole howse yarde were dyvers children englishe and dutche to the number of cth or vi score, all spynning of fyne bay yarne, a thing well lyked both of her majestie and of the nobilletie and ladies. And withowt the gate stode all the soldiers with their small shott, and upon the wall at the butts stode certen great peces, but the chambers by meane of the wetnes of the morninge could not be dischardged. The great peces were shot of and the small shott dischardged thryes. And at her departinge mr maior exhibited unto her highnes a supplicacion for the havon, which she tooke, and promised herself to reade.

My lord threasurer, my lord admyrall, my lord chamberleyn and my lord of Leycester, were made pryvie to the suyt for the havon; they lyked well thereof, and promised their furtheraunce' (W. Boys).[10]

**1586** This is one of the Cinque ports, as they are called, and is defended to the north and west by walls, on the other sides by a rampart, river, and ditch. It formerly felt the ravages of the Danes, and in the last age the fire of the French. It is now sufficiently populous, though the harbour by the sand driven in and a great merchant ship of Pope Paul IV, sunk in the very middle of it, is not capable of admitting large ships (W. Camden).[11]

**1602 (1st July)** Yesterday in the afternoon there was great lightning and thunder, with hailstones in many places of nine inches compass, which at Sandwich in Kent lay a foot deep on the ground, broke the glass windows of churches and tiles of houses. Some barns also were fired by lightning (Anon).[12]

**1621** We left Margate at 11 o'clock in the morning in good weather ... The ground was high and fertile, but we saw some very large cornfields ... From the heights a little further on there was on our left the most beautiful view in the world, straight ahead appeared a large inlet, from the sea and on a headland Deal or Downs, where a large English fleet and some Dutch ships lay at anchor, all along the coast from the North Foreland to the Downs, and on our right the rich pastures of Kent. We descended from the heights with Sandwich straight ahead of us and drove along the beach next to the sea. There were some fertile fields with blue pebbles and boulders as far as one could see ...

At 2 o'clock in the afternoon we got to Sandwich and went to the Dolphin Inn to refresh ourselves with their excellent beer, which they served up in 4 wooden tankards at a time. Sandwich is a medium size town, lying on a river, but besides the church there is not much of interest to be seen. We left there at 4 o'clock in a peculiar waggon drawn by four mules with bells on their heads, harnessed in single file; our commander, called John Haenbrouck, was on foot, an extremely funny fellow (who would have made a good clown) and his servant or boy Josaphat alias hang-ear, who made the way appear short with his funny stories and grimaces (W. Schellinks).[13]

**1635** Being mounted I posted away, ouer a little Riuer into a faire Island ... a Paradice of pleasant Meads and fertile Marishes, fruitfull and delightfull Fields of Corne ... after a short consultation with my Selfe, I suddenly fac'd to the right, and troop'd to a far better qualifyld Maritime Towne, this Limbs Head and one of the Cinque Parts of this Kingdome ... And at this place, after I was ferry'd ouer to the Key side, I thought it safer for me to rest in at that time than to goe on to seeke vncertain Quartering at Deale ... therefore accordingly I resolued to abide at this Towne of Sandwich and there to take my rest for that time.

Heere I found a pretty and well built Towne, both wall'd, and dik'd about, with 5 Gates, neere half a mile in length, and a quarter in breadth, and many fair Streets therein: and more especially one [Delfe Street] that runs all along in the middst of the Towne: there is a dainty sweet and cleare Riuolet about knee deepe, with Archt and pau'd Bridges ouer it to euery house, gliding through it. And another street [Strand Street] that runs along through the Towne neerer the Key, with many fayre streets that crosse thwart the same. There is a fayre Towne Hall in the Markett Place, A fayre Free schoole by Canterbury Gate, build by the late Lord Cheife Baron Manwood; small vessells come vp to the Key; A Bulwarke there is with some Ordinance, but much decay'd ... There is two Captaines that commaund the train'd Bands, made vp of the Inhabitants, who are in all 200, each Captaine hauing the Commaund of 100 men (Anon).[14]

**1665-1672.** To Sandwich, a pretty towne about 2 miles from the sea, a river: The country sandy: here the Mayor also very dilligent to serve me ... I came back through a Country the best cultivated of any that in my life I had anywhere seene, every field lying as even as a bowling greene, and the fences, plantations and husbandrie in such admirable order, as indefinitely delighted me. (J. Evelyn)[15]

1681 Sandwich was formerly more frequented by seamen when the haven and river were not so choked by sand, nevertheless hoys and some small ships do come up to the town, in the river that comes from Canterbury, which with the trade of malting, constantly employing some vessels towards London, keeps this place from decay. It is fortified with a deep trench and bulwarks of earth, but towards the sea some parts are walled. 'Tis beautified with three churches whose leaden spires at some distance, coming towards the town, seem to stand exactly in rank. On the North side almost a mile without the town is yet to be seen the ruins of a castle on a point of land formerly surrounded with the sea and serviceable in the days of Earl Goodwin. But now 'tis deserted by the sea which comes not within a mile or more of it (T. Baskerville).[16]

1693 Sandwich ... the most famous of all the Ports of England ... a place notable indeed for abundance of sand of each side of the Channel, whose banks sinus-like are of a winding, curving, and imbowed form and figure (W. Somner).[17]

1697 .... beyond Deale you go a very deepe heavy sand for 4 miles to Sandwich; you go along by the Sea side in sight of the Isle of Thannet which is just over against Sandwich ... this is a sad old town all timber building, you enter by a gate and so you go out of it by a gate, but its run so to decay that except one or two good houses its just like to drop down the whole town (C. Fiennes).[18]

**Georgian Sandwich.**

Although the legacy of the plague-ridden years of the seventeenth century was a slow rate of population increase, this set-back was largely offset by a series of developments which precipitated a return of prosperity to Sandwich. While the town's population and industrial base remained limited in size and ambition, its mercantile sector proved highly responsive to the opportunities opening up before it. Indeed, the insatiable demand for foodstuffs in London and the burgeoning towns of the Medway valley and Thames estuary led to a boom in the town's coasting trade with these markets. The rich agricultural lands of East Kent produced enormous quantities of wheat, barley, hops, fruit and vegetables, and the bulk of this produce was shipped out of the region via Sandwich. Other important developments also contributed much to the town's advance, in particular, the turnpiking of the roads to the east of Canterbury, such as those leading to Sandwich, Dover and the Isle of

Thanet, helped to bring an end to the town's isolation and integrate it into the wider world. The linking of the turnpiked roads of East Kent to those of West Kent encouraged long-distance east-west travel between the two halves of the county, while the inauguration of a regular stage-coach and carrier service between London and Sandwich brought rising numbers of travellers to the town. All these activities brought wealth and prosperity to Sandwich, and this manifests itself in a number of ways; in the remodelling of dwellings in the better-off streets, such as Fisher Street and High Street, in the paving and cleansing of the streets, and in the opening of an Assembly Room, Theatre and Book Club in the town.

**1719** This Place hath formerly been a strong Town, being to this Day Walled on the North and West sides, and on the others is defended with a Rampart and Ditch ... But the Sand at the Mouth by degrees choaking up the Haven, it soon after fell into a State of Decay; and had done so much sooner, but that it was in a good Measure supported by the Walloons, and other Protestant Refugees, who here set up, the first of any in England, publick Gardening, Sowing Canary-Seeds, etc. and by that Means kept the Town from running to Ruin. But it is now a very poor Place; though still famous for Carrots, Beans, Artichokes, etc., and indeed the Soil is very good for all Sorts of Garden-Stuff (J. Harris).[19]

**1723** This stream [the Stour] is still so deep that it serves for Lighters to go on it to and fro from Fordwich to Sandwich with Coals, Deal-boards and other such Heavy carriage (J. Lewis).[20]

**1724** Sandwich is the next town, lying in the bottom of a bay, at the mouth of the river Stour, an old, decay'd, poor, miserable town, of which when I have said that it is an antient town, one of the Cinque Ports, and sends two members to Parliament; I have said all that I think can be worth any bodies reading of the town of Sandwich (D. Defoe).[21]

**1749** Peace proclaimed, on the 11th of feb. 1749, in the middle of the corn market, at the pump in the fish market, and on the top of pelican hill. The procession was made in the following order. Two constables; a troop of dragoons on horseback; the rest of the constables and the deputies four and four; seamen with colors; a band of music; the three sergeants at mace in their gowns on horseback; the mayor and townclerk, the jurats two and two, in their gowns on horseback; the common councilmen on horseback; the cordwainers company and the mercers company on foot; the ensigns of the militia with their colors on horseback; the four militia drums, and the eight sergeants on horseback with their halberds; gentlemen of the town on horseback two and two. The bells rung, and all the houses were adorned with green boughs. The order of the procession was formed in the corn market by taking a circuit round the court hall and cross house, and proceeding from thence at the east side of the fish market to the pump, and returning along the west side of the fish market to the corner of the corn market, and so up new street round the chain into high street to pelican hill, and from thence proceeding through strand street and harnet street to the corn market, which finished the procession. Then mr mayor, the jurats and gentlemen went to the court hall, and drank the health of his majesty and the royal family &c, under a discharge of the cannon round the town walls; and in the evening the whole town was illuminated; bonfires &c (W. Boys).[22]

**1754** Sandwich is pleasantly situated on the river ... The town of Sandwich was defended on the side of the river, and to the gate at each end by a wall and towers, and at the east end by a large tower called the Bulwark, which is now in ruins. The other parts of the town are fortyfied only by a strong rampart, the town not being above a quarter of a mile broad. There are a great number of old houses in it, mostly built with wooden frames, and a fine stream runs through the town. It rose out of the ruins of Rutupiae. The harbour is now bad, being choaked up with sand ... The chief support of the town is an export of malt, and an import of wine and other forreign commodities for the use of Canterbury and other neighbouring towns. They also send a great quantity of garden seeds and carrots to London (R. Pocock).[23]

**C.1760** I do not know whether I have told you that I am a subscriber to the Sandwich Assembly, with which I am greatly delighted. It was with some reluctance that I went at first, but now I am so well pleased with it that I shall go as often as I can. You may imagine I find something very engaging in it, that I can overcome my indolence so far as to go five miles, and lie a whole night out of my own dear chamber (E. Carter).[24]

**1776** [I found] ... more hope for the poor people than I had done for many years [in] ... poor dry, dead Sandwich (J. Wesley).[25]

**1776** Sandwiche ... is a turning river in a sandy soil (T. Philipott).[26]

**1783** Got up about six, sett off for Dover at eight. Came to Sandwich, which on the outside look to be a very pretty, neat town but was a very disagreeable, dirty town. We cam through a wooden drawbridge for which we paid 1s. 6d., which we thought was a very unreasonable toll. The Streets are narrow & not paved. The road was not a turnpike Road but a very good one. We supposed the country round to be very fine but it was so thick, we could not see it (M. Coke).[27]

**1788**     Sandwich...one of the most disagreeable towns I ever saw, the streets so narrow there is not room for two carriages to pass, the houses poor and miserable (M. Coke).[28]

**1789**     Being quite hoarse, I could neither sing nor speak: however, I determined to show myself, at least, where I had appointed to preach. Coming to Sandwich about noon, and finding the congregation was waiting, I trusted in God, and began to speak: the more I spoke, the more my voice was strengthened; so that in a few minutes I think all could hear; and many, I believe, took knowledge that what they heard was not the word of man, but of God (J. Wesley).[29]

**1792**     Sandwich ... is five miles from Deal by the horse road through the sand hills, and about seven by the coach road through Ham and Finglesham... the depth of the water at the mouth of the harbour at ordinary spring tides is about 14 or 15 feet, and sometimes, when the wind blows strong from the north west ... the water has risen there to the height of 20 feet. The perpendicular rise of the water at Sandwich bridge, in common spring tides, is about 8 feet, and the whole depth of water is then about 14 feet.... the exports from Sandwich are corn, grain, flour, seeds, hops, wool, malt, apples, pears, leather, oak bark, ashes, &c. - the imports grocery, furniture, linen, woollen and other shop goods from London; iron, plank, spars, timber, lead, Scotch and Welsh coal, salt, wine, spirits, porter, glass, grindstones, portland and other stone &c from Wales, Scotland, Sweden, Norway and the Baltic.... The soil about Sandwich to the eastward is a deep sandy loam, and the land there was by the Dutch settlers wholly appropriated to the growth of esculent plants, legumens and seeds. These perhaps were the first gardens for the supply of public markets in the kingdom. Some parts of the ground are applied to the same use now; but the greater portion is in tillage for corn. The lands to the south consist of a deep rich soil, which is highly fertilized by the application of manure from the town, and by the deposit from the smoke of the coal fires, which very soon sullies the fleeces of sheep that are brought into pastures near the town (W. Boys).[30]

**1793**     I ought not to quit Betshanger without mentioning the pleasure I had of dining with Mr. Boys, at the Sandwich Book Club, at that town; when I had the satisfaction of finding a very numerous company, perfectly loyal in their conversation, their toasts, and their songs. The presence of Paine served, when here (and he was here on his way to France), only to raise sentiments of contempt and abhorrence. He changed the hisses of the English for the applauses of the French, which have not yet finished with the sabre or the halter (A. Young).[31]

King Street

**1794**     The walls of the town ... are nearly in the form of a parallelogram, and are about five furlongs in length from east to west, and two and a half from north to south; at the foot of which is a wet ditch of considerable breadth. They command a pleasant and extensive view of the adjacent country. In these walls are several semicircular projections which overlook the ditches, there were also some pieces of ordnance, which being quite unserviceable, have been lately removed.... It appears, from the remains of fortifications about this town, that it was anciently a place of great strength, and before the use of cannon, was capable of enduring a vigorous siege.

The river is now about thirty yards broad at high water, over which travellers, horses and carriages, were conveyed in a flat-bottom boat ... in the year 1756 ... the present bridge was begun; and finished in the following year ... The bridge is built with stone, having an arch on each side, and a passage between for the larger vessels that use this port. The middle arch is wood, divided into two parts, which are hung nearly in an equilibrium, by which means they are easily drawn up or let down. The passage over the stone part of the bridge is secured by a parapet wall on each side, and the wooden arch by Chinese rails. It is a work of considerable utility, not only to the inhabitants of Sandwich and the Isle of Thanet, but to the eastern parts of the county of Kent, and the public in general; the ferry having been much inconvenient and dangerous, and no small obstruction to trade.

The streets of Sandwich are narrow and irregular. Strand street, which reaches from west to east, might have been made a commodious throughfare; but at present is broken into many disagreeable angles. High street, Fisher street, and Delph street, are the broadest and most airy, in which are several good houses. Here is a handsome square called the Fish-market, which consists principally of shops; but the avenues leading to it are indifferent, excepting that from the Corn-market, which is another square, much larger than the former, but inferior to it with respect to the buildings.

The trade of this town chiefly consists in coal, fir timber, deals etc., with which the country is supplied. Here also are shipped corn, malt, fruit, and seeds for London and other markets. The seeds raised from this soil are in much repute. ... The shrimps which are caught near this town are remarkably excellent. There are several good inns in Sandwich, and many wealthy inhabitants. Here is also a large and elegant assembly room, which has been built within these few years. Since the construction of the bridge, and the resort to Margate as a bathing place, the town has been more frequently visited by strangers; a tour from thence to Sandwich, Deal, Dover, etc., being a pleasant and agreeable excursion (T. Fisher).[32]

**1794**  In the vicinity of Sandwich there are a great many orchards, which some years produce large quantities of excellent apples; some of which go to the London market, but the principal part is sent by coal vessels to Sunderland and Newcastle.

The farmers usually sell their orchard by the lump to fruiterers, who gather, sort, and pack them, in baskets, or old sugar hogsheads, for exportation (J. Boys).[33]

**1800**  From its exceeding low situation, on what was once the bed of the sea, bounded by the present haven, or creek, on one side, and a vast quantity of wet and damp marshes on the other sides of it, this town cannot possibly be healthy, or even a desirable place of habitation. It is in shape an oblong square; the houses are old fashioned and ill built, and the streets, which are in general but narrow and ill-convenient lanes, little adapted either for carriages or even horses; an exception to this, however, is High-street, which is of good breadth, and much better built ... At the entrance of the town from Canterbury, is the grammar school. In the centre of the town, near St. Peter's church, is the market or butchery, and near the south part of it, the cattle and fish markets, and close to them the guild, or town hall ... The town is not well supplied with good water; the springs lie high, and fill the wells with very indifferent water; but there is every where, at the depth of from forty to fifty-eight feet, a stratum of flint, which ... yields a plentiful supply of fine water; but as the land drains are not kept out of the wells by steening, the inhabitants have not that advantage they would otherwise have from them. The other supplies are from the haven and the delf, which is an artificial stream or canal, raised in some parts above the level of the grounds through which it runs ... The soil about Sandwich, to the eastward, is a deep sandy loam ... and Canterbury and Dover markets, are still in good measure supplied from them, where the garden stuff and seeds, carried from hence, bear the preference of any others, especially the carrots, and are distinguished by the name of Sandwich carrots ... The exports at this haven are now confined to the products of the neighbouring country for a few miles round, and the imports mostly to shop goods, and other necessary articles for the town and the adjoining country; for which purpose there are several hoys, which sail to and from London, though there are a few ships of larger size, which at times make voyages as far as Wales, Scotland, Sweden, Norway, and the Baltic (E. Hasted).[34]

**Regency and Victorian Sandwich.**

Unlike the industrial towns of north-west Kent, which experienced an economic and demographic transformation during the nineteenth century, Sandwich continued to remain an old-fashioned market town with a near static population and a limited industrial base. Although the century began on a promising note, as the Anglo-French wars of 1793-1815 stimulated employment and incomes in the town, the ending of the hostilities brought the good times to an emphatic end and ushered in a recession that lasted until at least the middle of the century. As the demand for shipping, provisions and naval equipment fell away, a number of victualling towns and ports such as Deal and Sandwich, whose livelihood depended on servicing the warships in the Downs, suffered a notable rise in the level of unemployment and social misery, thus compelling the Poor Law authorities to relieve those rendered destitute by the recession. At the same time the town's coasting trade continued to be limited by the shallow waters of the Stour. To some extent this limitation on trade was overcome in1847 when the town, following the building of a branch line between Minster and Deal, was linked to the Kentish railway network. Bulky raw materials such as coal, timber and building materials, and certain luxury consumer goods that were not readily available in East Kent, continued to be imported from London and elsewhere. A certain amount of overseas trade was also conducted with Holland, Norway and Sweden. The coming of the railway to Sandwich not only encouraged greater physical mobility for those who could afford the fares, but it also attracted rising numbers of tourists to the town.

**1815** The Country about here is very open plenty of corn. We stopped some time at Sandwich a very pretty little place with a nice Large Church. Just out of the village is a pretty little river and further on are the Salt pits, square places in which they make Salt (T. Lot).[35]

**1818** The town of Sandwich, whether considered as a sea-port to which title it has lost almost all pretensions ... exhibits, perhaps, less appearance of commerce, or manufactures, or amusement, or gaiety, than any other town of equal size in the kingdom. Indeed it is extremely difficult to convey any adequate idea of the contrast which is here afforded to the crowded streets and busy hum which usually characterize a maritime town: the contrast between Sandwich, before the destruction of its harbour and port, and its present state, where dulness seems to have established an undisturbed reign. It would scarcely give too high a colouring to the picture, if a walk through this ancient town were compared to the solemn sadness of a visit to Herculaneum or Pompeia. At present besides its narrow but well-paved streets, its decayed walls and gates, its dismal and dilapidated churches and the narrow channel of the Stour, into which a few small vessels only find a passage from the sea, now at two miles' distance, little remains to supply materials for description.

Deal affords a complete contrast to Sandwich. On visiting the latter, a stranger, as he wanders solitary through the town, in which the pavement dreads the turf's encroaching green, and scarcely a human being is visible even at noon-day, will be induced to ask, Where are the inhabitants? But as soon as he arrives at Deal, he is surrounded by so great a throng as to obstruct his passage along the streets, and is tempted to exclaim, Where can such a multitude find habitations? (J. Fussell)[36]

1818   Sandwich is very irregularly built, and has an appearance of greater antiquity, perhaps, than any other town in this county, ... Great part of the Walls yet remain; and till within the last thirty-five years, there were five of the ancient Gates standing also (E. Brayley).[37]

1822   Sandwich is a most irregularly built town, and has more appearances of age than perhaps any other in Kent ... A very considerable portion of the ancient Walls of the town is yet remaining. Its general antique appearance has been noticed; and it may be observed, that the streets and lanes are mostly narrow and inconvenient; though some considerable improvements have been made under an Act, passed in 1787, for new paving, lighting, watching, and cleansing the place (T. Cromwell).[38]

1823   I got to this place about half an hour after the ringing of the eight o'clock bell, or Curfew, which 1 heard at about two miles distance from the place ... From Deal you come along to Upper Deal ... thence upon a beautiful road to Sandwich, which is a rotten Borough. Rottenness, putridity is excellent for land, but bad for Boroughs. This place, which is as villanous a hole as one would wish to see, is surrounded by some of the finest land in the world. Along on one side of it, lies a marsh. On the other sides of it is land which they tell me bears seven quarters of wheat to an acre. It is certainly very fine; for I saw large pieces of radish-seed on the road side; this seed is grown for the seedsmen in London; and it will grow on none but rich land. All the corn is carried here except for some beans and some barley. ... In quitting Sandwich, you immediately cross a river up which vessels bring coals from the sea. This marsh is about a couple of miles wide ... I had to cross this river, and to cross the marsh, before I got into the famous Isle of Thanet ... Soon after crossing the river, I passed by a place for making salt ... On the marsh I found the same sort of sheep as on Romney Marsh; but the cattle here are chiefly Welsh; black, and called runts. They are nice hardy cattle ... When I got upon the corn land in the Isle of Thanet, I got into a garden indeed (W. Cobbett).[39]

| 1823 | Sandwich seems a clean town, it used to be fortified, there is an old gateway on the Canterbury road (C. Powell).[40] |
|---|---|
| 1824 | Sandwich Haven, in its present state, is difficult of ingress and egress; hence vessels have frequently been off the Port several days, and even weeks, without being able to enter it, and others have been detained a yet greater space of time in the Haven, in consequence of being unable to get out of it; and it seldom happens that vessels get out of, or enter the Harbour, without being detained by obstacles, which, by the assistance of a steam boat, would be easily surmounted ... Again, vessels, after having entered the River, are frequently detained several days before they can get up to the Town, and when they are bound out, they are in like manner detained several tides, before they can get down the River, and to get either up or down it, they are obliged to employ men to track them, at a charge of at least 1s. per ton. A Steam Boat might tow such vessels from sea up to the Town, and from the Town to the sea, at a charge of six-pence per ton (W. Pettman).[41] |
| 1824 | The trade of this town has been considerable in corn, malt, hops, timber, iron, coals, salt, &c. for which it offers great facility, being situated at the mouth of the river Stour, which here empties itself into Sandwich haven, and is navigable by barges to Canterbury. The market days are Wednesday and Saturday; on the former of these a very considerable corn market is held, and every alternate Monday there is a well supplied cattle market, both of which are remarkably well attended. There are some minor fairs, and a considerable one on the 4th of December, which often lasts ten days, when the theatre is open and various amusements carried on (Pigot and Co.).[42] |
| 1831 | Sandwich is a dull. deserted Town, with little prospect of improving its decayed condition. It is washed on the north-east by the river Stour, and surrounded on every other side by a dyke, the remains of its old fortifications. The river takes a very circuitous course, and at a short distance below Sandwich approaches very closely to its bed above the town. At this spot, called Salterns, a sluice has been cut for the purpose of relieving the lands near Canterbury; and although that object has been fully attained, the result has been very injurious to the navigation at Sandwich, in consequence of the discharge of the water through the more direct channel (Boundary Commissioners).[43] |
| 1832 | The foreign trade of Sandwich is principally with Norway, Sweden, and the Baltic, for timber and iron; and the home trade with Wales and Scotland, in flour, seeds, hops, malt, fruit, &c. Ship building and rope |

making are carried on to a limited extent, but there are no vestiges of its ancient woollen trade existing. The Bell Inn is the principal posting house, and it is also the chief one resorted to by the commercial traveller (Pigot and Co.).[44]

1834　This place has fallen off even more than Deal since the peace; and in St. Peter's parish, 24 houses are now empty; the ship-yard is broken up, the malting business abandoned, and such is the general poverty, that they are not able to do even what they wish for the poor. In St. Mary's parish, out of 900 persons, 600 receive constant or occasional relief. There are two workhouses ... Complaint is here made of the ill effect of the local jurisdiction; members of the corporation are elected by the poorer class of inhabitants: hence there is a tendency in the magistrates to lean to paupers whose votes may be useful in securing their election; freemen meet with favour and non-freemen must receive relief also, to keep up the semblance of impartiality (Poor Law Commissioners).[45]

1835　The town is very dull, and has little or no trade of any kind. The best houses let for about £35, and many of them are uninhabited. There are two or three tan-yards in full employ, and in the course of the year a good deal of wool is sorted and sent off to various parts. A project has long been entertained of making a harbour near the mouth of the river, and shortening the navigation to Canterbury by means of canals. This would benefit Sandwich greatly, but there seems to be no probability of its being carried into execution (Municipal Commissioners).[46]

1837　We think it high time that the authorities of Sandwich should look into the state of public thoroughfares as there is scarcely a street but is actually dangerous for a carriage to travel on through the sad repair they are kept in; in almost all parts of the town may be seen lumps of mortar, bricks and other rubbish lying for nights together, to the imminent risk of travellers. What can the street surveyor be about? (Kent Herald).[47]

1838　Sandwich .... is built upon the River Stour .... the harbour has become so insignificant, as hardly to deserve the name of a harbour at all. What remains of it is now, if the distance be measured by the windings of the shrunken stream, three or four miles below the town, and the water almost stagnates in a heavy bed of still accumulating sand (C. Greenwood).[48]

1838　This town can scarcely be regarded as a Watering Place, although at a small distance accommodations for sea bathing have been provided. ... The town is irregularly built on the south bank of the Stour, in which many vestiges evince that the sea once flowed over the present valley of the river. The sea is now distant from the town about a mile and a half in a right line, or four miles and a half by the course of the haven, which is navigable to the heart of the town for vessels of from one hundred and fifty to two hundred tons burden, and in consequence enjoys a considerable inland trade; though it must be confessed, that since the invention of steam-vessels and rail-roads, other districts have silently diverted commerce into different channels, and many more modern places have superseded Sandwich, as she herself supplanted her neighbour Rutupiae. ... For the education of the poor children of the town, an excellent charity school has been established for upwards of one hundred years, supported by voluntary subscriptions ... Within these last three years, an excellent gaol has been erected at the outskirts of the town ... It is ... constructed more for use than ornament, and is capable of holding and classing from twenty to thirty prisoners. A treadwheel has been erected within the walls; and the greatest order, industry, and morality, are strictly maintained ... The town was formerly well walled in and surrounded with defences on all sides. Almost all the masonry composing these has been destroyed. But one of the gates ... Fishers' Gate is [still] standing, and is a picturesque object for the artist or the antiquary ... And though the visitor may regret the absence of these objects which conferred strength, beauty and security to the town, there can be little doubt ... that the health of the town has materially improved since their demolition, combined as it has been with the admirable system of irrigation pursued by the landed proprietors during the late war ... and the high state of cultivation in which the land in the neighbourhood was brought.

To the tourist on pleasure, or the casual observer, the town of Sandwich may present a locality apparently unfavourable to health; but a more minute enquiry, and scrutiny of the registers of mortality ... will utterly remove any such impression ... nor are those complaints which often affect the health of the residents of the valley in the vicinity of marshes (agues and febrile infections) common at Sandwich, though considerable tracts of marsh-land are to be found in the neighbourhood. Lands of the most fertile character, and in the highest possible state of cultivation, surround it (Anon).[49]

**1843** The town of Sandwich ... is situated on the south-eastern coast of England, about two miles in a direct line from the shore of that part of the British channel that is denominated the Downs. The site of the present partially irregular streets and buildings constitutes a tolerably uniform plane, gradually sloping towards the north and north-west, until it terminates on the bank of the river Stour, which has its course parallel to the remains of one portion of the antique walls, and separates the locality from the Isle of Thanet in that direction. As we approach the sea on the east and south-east

*The Cattle Market*

a considerable tract of downland interposes, the surface of which, at first moderately undulating, at length forms occasional sharp ridges and groups of sand-hills, which latter crowd upon shore, and by their broken and uncertain outline operate materially to intercept and circumscribe the view towards the horizon on this side of Sandwich. Over these hillocks and sand-downs, at certain seasons, the bleak northeast and easterly winds, after traversing the German ocean and Channel sea, sweep with singular rigidity ... Although the immediate neighbourhood of Sandwich abounds in rural scenery, consisting of timber trees, stump willows, tall poplars, and plantations of firs, larches, &c, very little foliage of any kind occurs within the walls of the town ... This now somewhat sequestered place, once a position of no small importance, and long since noted by historians for some curious remains of antiquity, contains three spacious churches, two only of which possess the appendage of a tower, or other claims of architectural distinction; the third being remarkable merely for its low, broad roof of extraordinary span, and an interior of corresponding dimensions. The tower of St. Peter, which is closely surrounded by numerous buildings intersected by several lines of principal thoroughfare, has its site not far removed from the nearly central market-place, and commands from its summit an extensive view over the adjacent country, as well as Thanet, the Downs, and, occasionally, under favourable atmospheric conditions, the opposite coast of France. The church of St. Clement is situated on the highest ground within the walls, and only a few yards distant from the remains of a deep and very ancient fosse, on the southeastern side of the town. The tower of this edifice presents various features of great masonic beauty, and is supposed to be one of the oldest Saxon buildings now remaining in England; it is, consequently, an object of great interest to the antiquary (Dr. W. Weekes).[50]

**1845** The town is irregularly built, but is paved and lighted. The streets are narrow; part of the town wall is still standing and of the Fishergate. The trade consists of tanning and wool sorting, in the importation of timber and iron, and the export of corn, malt, flour, seeds, hops, fruits, and wool (Post Office Directory).[51]

**1847** Wednesday and Saturday are the market days, the former for corn which is numerously attended by the farmers of the surrounding district. A cattle market is held every alternate Monday, and a fair for drapery, shoes, hardware and pedlery, commences annually on the 4th of December, and continues for a week. Assemblies are occasionally held during the season, in a spacious room at the Bell Inn, Strand-street ...The South Eastern Railway Station is about a quarter of a mile south from the town. Trains are despatched nine times a day to London, with the exception of Sunday, when they leave five times during the day. The Gaol is a substantial building ... It contains convenient arrangements for the classification of prisoners, and is provided with a tread-wheel (S. Bagshaw).[52]

1850  Sandwich is a place of great antiquity ... The streets are narrow, and part of the town wall is still standing. Although many families of substance and respectability reside in Sandwich, it wears a neglected and antique appearance, that carries us back to the time of the Tudors (Anon).[53]

1858  Many of the houses are ancient and irregularly built, and the streets are narrow and incommodious ... There is a Mechanics Institution, also a small theatre, a market-place where the grass springs freshly (G. Measom).[54]

1859  The railroad from Deal to Minster passes through Sandwich, a decayed town .... The ancient earthworks, like a wall, at once strike the visitor's eye on leaving the station, and the whole appearance of the quaint old place gives promise of a picturesque interior. The streets are narrow and grass grown; the Stour is still eleven feet deep and fifty feet broad at spring tide, but the harbour is choked with sand .... The corn-field flourishes close beneath the ramparts [of Richborough Castle]. The ash and wild trees pierce through the fissured walls, which are clad with creeping plants. Under the broken heaps of masonry flows a narrow river down to the dreary shore and marshes, where the fields of long tasselled reed grass ... murmur in the wind and ripple over like a wavy sea; where, too, dyke and channel yet remain to show the labour of the monks. In the rents of the once strong bastion ... the farmer now lays his ploughshare and the wandering gipsy shelters from the storm (M. Walcott).[55]

1859  There is a corn market held every Wednesday at the Fleur de Lis and an extensive cattle market every alternate Monday, and a yearly pleasure fair on the 4th December... The town is irregularly built, but is paved and lighted with gas. Many of the streets are narrow; part of the town wall is still standing, and a portion of the Fishergate. The trade of the town consists chiefly of tanning, wool sorting, and ship building, and in the importation of coal, timber, and iron, and export of corn, malt, flour, seeds, hops, fruit, and wool. Here are an iron foundry, breweries, malting houses, a ship-building yard, and a seed-crushing mill. It possesses considerable advantages and facilities for commerce, enjoying both water traffic and direct railway communication with London; its importation of coal is very extensive, supplying the large agricultural district around.

Sandwich is situated in the midst of a wide area of rich marsh land, through which the river Stour bends its course to Pegwell bay and the sea... Sandwich now enjoys the advantages of direct railway and telegraphic communication with the metropolis and intermediate places. The journey to London is accomplished in a little more than three hours. There are likewise hoys which sail weekly between Wool quay, Lower Thames-street, London, and Sandwich (Kelly's Directory).[56]

**1863** Without anything very picturesque about it, the town has a strangely old-world and Plantagenet character. The streets and houses are so crushed together, and so intricate, and there is such an entire absence of all novelty, that the general impression is very great. It much resembles the less architectural parts of Bruges - a likeness increased by its large and numerous churches ... The morass below the town is still called the Haven; and through it the Stour winds so greatly that its course is nearly 4m. in length before reaching the sea. Still vessels of 200 tons come up to the bridges, and a considerable number of small craft is built there ... The walls towards the river were of stone, the others of earth. Along these a broad path has been made, affording curious views over the town; which, with its garden spaces and drying fields, recalls the views of old Flemish cities illustrating Guicciardini's folio (J. Murray).[57]

**1865** From foreign enemies the desertion of the sea has long since secured [Sandwich] ... The approach to Sandwich from the west must have reminded many ... of those old Flemish pictures of which in earlier days, and at the period when it was the resort of so many sojourners from the Low Countries, it must have frequently formed the subject. The marshes of the foreground, the familiar mills on the left, and the two churches crowning the landscape, one of which, in its hard outline and quaint ogee cupola, looks almost an importation from Holland - a kind of Dutch bulb - must bring to mind very forcibly the long connection of the Cinque Ports with the havens of the Flemish coast; while the broad and impressive Norman tower of St. Clement's, the beautiful arcading of which becomes the most prominent feature of the town as we approach it more nearly, carries us back to a more distant past ... Sandwich represents the strange anomaly of a port without a haven, or fortress without fortifications, a perfect code of trading without a trade ... Sandwich, once wedded to the sea like Venice, and now so strangely divorced from it, is sinking into feebleness and obscurity.... (R. Jenkins).[58]

**1867** There is much to interest the antiquarian at Sandwich... Sandwich is united to Stonar and the Isle of Thanet by a bridge, the centre of which opens for the passage of vessels having stationary masts. The river at spring tides is about 50 feet in width, and in some places 11 feet deep. From its contiguity to the marshes, the town is not considered healthy. The houses are quaint and primitive, and mostly of an ordinary description; the streets, with the

Sailing barges on the Quay, in the late nineteenth century

exception of High Street, although well paved, resemble lanes, and are ill-suited for carriage traffic ... Here the busy hum of its once crowded streets has lapsed into repose, and the jostlings of active life, lost in painful quiet, sadly contrast with its former glory and importance (W. Miller).[59]

**1874** So dull, so aged is the aspect of its quiet curious streets one would not be surprised to meet there a trooper of King Charles's times. Decaying trade, a stagnant social life, a dearth of anything like public spirit, a drowsy stupid contentment with things as they are ... have slowly but surely undermined the position of this once important town (D. Gardiner).[60]

**1874** We now push on to Sandwich, and enter the town ... A strange old town - a sort of memorial to the dead England of the feudal days - a motionless, sleepy town, which seems to have been suddenly disinterred from its years-long grave, and not to have thoroughly roused itself into life and action! "Some half-dozen vessels of moderate burden," says a graphic writer, "are seen on each side as you cross the bridge, and you take it for granted that within the town there will be the bustle usual in a seaport". Instead of this, however, there is a lifeless quiet, more marked than in many a country village of the smallest size and most sequestered situation. Unless on a market morning (which occurs once in a fortnight), you may walk from end to end of the long dreary High Street, and scarcely meet an individual; and if you meet one he is sauntering listlessly along as if there were nothing in the world for him to be doing. Still, Sandwich is hardly a place that a stranger would pass an hour in without wishing to know something more about. The streets are narrow and irregular, the houses generally rude, mean, and low; but then the streets cover a considerable space, the houses many of them are old, and appear to have been of a better grade, and the churches shew signs of having belonged to a more important place, and a more active population than they now do. Something more of life and business has, however, been flung into the town, and galvanized it into a show of activity, by its communication with "the outer world" being improved. All honour to the railway! ... Few towns in England have undergone a greater and more striking change than Sandwich. It is now two miles from the sea, and the river on which it stands is scarcely navigable for ships of very small burthen; and yet it was formerly one of the wealthiest of our English ports. The marsh below the town is still called The Haven, but the Stour meanders through it in so sinuous a course that its mouth is four miles distant from the town (A. Black).[61]

**1876** To this day ... the quaint, foreign-looking aspect of the place never fails to strike the visitor with surprise (S. Smiles).[62]

*Strand Street in the late nineteenth century*

**1881** There is a large timber yard, a tannery, a large corn store, and two breweries. The principal and substantial trade is upon the river; there are considerable imports of timber, coals, and corn in the course of the year. It supplies a large part of the district with coal ... there is an iron foundry and things of that kind upon a moderate scale (Commissioners of Corrupt Practices).[63]

**1881** ... they are pretty artful in Sandwich; they are not fools there; they are very artful people, very cunning and very close (Commissioners of Corrupt Practices).[64]

**1887** This ancient town... is now some 4m. distant from the sea (following the course of the river) and so difficult of access that only comparatively small craft can reach it. In keeping with the decay of the port, the town itself has become so stagnant that the grass is said to grow in some of the streets. But apart from its commercial dulness, it is an interesting place, both for old associations and present remains ... The town was surrounded by walls, of which a considerable portion still exists, formed into a pleasant open walk, bordered by planted slopes, very much resembling a Belgian or Flemish town (G. Bevan).[65]

**1888** Arrested at a certain stage of decadence, a moderately old world still confronts the visitor. One or two old gates survive to tell the story of the later Middle Ages: the noble tower of St. Clement's proclaims the grandeur of the early times: a few barges at the river-quay prove the existence of life; and over the marshy land you may see the lofty sails of one or two more, apparently sailing opposite ways, but engaged in making their tedious nine-miles course by the many-winding reaches of the Stour to that faithless sea (M. Burrows).[66]

**1889** Figure yourself in a sailing boat proceeding from Ramsgate to Deal; as you open that small space of waters called Pegwell Bay, your eye is invited by a prospect of mud, stretching slimily into sand at the extremity of whose flat and barren reaches you see a few trees with a church top or two showing above or amongst them. It is Sandwich, once a flourishing little seaport, when the salt surge of the Channel washed close to its gates; now a stranded borough, left high and dry by old time; as bleak and melancholy a wreck as any row of ship's ribs that ever grinned upon the yellow line of the Goodwins right abreast of us out there. The moral atmosphere of this aged place is most uncomfortably suggestive of the past. A flavour of death and of dust haunts it. There is a surprising lifelessness in the aspect of its houses. Unless you walk warily, you may perchance stumble over some ancient tombstone that has impertinently thrust itself beyond the consecrated precincts, or that, like the town itself, has been left aground by the ebbing of the wall or fence that once enclosed it. The inhabitants flit ghost-like from pavement to pavement. The few shops, cavernous in character and sunk in gloom, suggest themselves as the resort of the spirits of the tradesmen over whose graves in the adjacent churchyards the green, weather-swept and indecipherable tombstones lean feebly as though the next gale of wind must level them. It needs a powerful imagination to figure this silent, motionless old borough as once full of the noise of business, its streets enriched by the colour of frequent pageants, its air clamourous with the songs and cries of mariners, the clear water, washing to it, reflecting the tall sides and the gay flags of armed ships of burthen... As you enter it nowadays, crossing the bridge over the dingy little river that washes the keels of the few small colliers and barges which find their way through the mud of Pegwell Bay up the Channel of the Stour to as high as the town in tow of the most rickety little tug that eye ever beheld, you find it very hard indeed to realize amid the grass and stillness of the streets that again and again in the vanished centuries the walls of the houses have re-echoed the acclamations of crowds assembled to witness the arrival of high and mighty princes, monarchs of our own country, sovereigns and potentates from abroad (W. Russell).[67]

**1890** There is a quiet beauty about its close clustered red roofs and quaint towers ... which few English towns can equal, and which one must go to Holland to find anything to surpass ... In the town itself, the quaint and winding streets, the old gabled and over-hanging houses, and the many picturesque 'bits' which meet one at every turn, all combine ... to make it not an unreasonable piece of advice to all who are in search of quiet, health, rest or artistic or literary inspiration to - try Sandwich (G. Griffin).[68]

**1894** I am making a summer holiday excursion about a corner of the pastoral county of Kent and come upon the quaint, old-fashioned port of Sandwich. I am impressed with the remarkable way in which it has retired from the sea, gone inland, as it were, like a migrated city; gone inland, nursing its strange history and traditions ... its commercial and social disappointments, and retiring altogether from a seafaring life. I wander about the old place and note the curious waterways, that wind through the town, forming natural moats to streets and houses. An odd little town, it has crept within the shadow of Progress and business ... Sandwich has literally migrated. The men who knew it as a port and harbour would seek it in vain. They would come ashore ... and find meadow-lands covered with sheep ... dykes and watercourses; they would come upon an old highway where their ships had ridden at anchor ... but no Sandwich would meet their eager gaze. They would see a narrow, sluggish river creeping from the sea through miles of daisy-dotted lands, velvety green. Inquiring their way in the direction of a square church tower in the distance, some two miles from the sea, they would find the remains of the lost city, right away in the country, on the banks of that creek-like river of salt and mud, which, with a stray brig or barque floating lazily on the tide, represents the only living reminiscences of the days when Sandwich was a famous port.

One of the peculiarities of this migrated port and town is the water- supply. ... Sandwich rejoices in a freshwater river that runs in and out of the old streets in the pleasantest fashion. It is always clear, fresh, and two or three feet in depth, and it constitutes the water-supply of the town. Now it runs along a street, by doorways and under bow-windows, skirting the side-walk, and rippling a constant song of delight. Here and there it pauses to supply a pump, or to answer the claims of buckets, brought down flights of steps connected with ancient houses. Then it will slip away under some old tunnel, to dash out again by green lawns and gardens, and to reappear in the quiet streets. The authorities of the town lead it hither and thither, confining it within stone walls, and tempting it through culverts. Once it pauses and swells out into a little pond for horses to drink at; but that is after its purer stream is locked up against the contamination of sea-water and the befoulment of a tanner who cleanses his skins in it, just before it joins that sluggish reminiscence of the sea ... (J. Hatton).[69]

**1897** There is stealing over us an exposition of sleep, which in Sandwich no one has been able to resist. Sandwich itself is drowsy. There is a soothing murmur of dozing life, and we shall gradually fall into a Sandwich sleep, to wake up like two Rip van Winkles fifty years after, only to find Sandwich just as it was when we went to sleep at the close of the nineteenth century (F. Burnand).[70]

## Twentieth Century Sandwich.

Until the outbreak of the Second World War the general pace of life in Sandwich closely resembled that of the previous century. To the delight of the many travellers who visited the town, Sandwich continued to retain its old-world character. As in earlier times, the town's population, which stood at 3,246 in 1931, increased at an imperceptible rate, whilst its industrial structure, like that of most other small country market towns at that time, consisted of a limited number of small-scale family-run firms and one-man retail outlets. In Sandwich, brewing, malting, leather tanning, fruit packing and the retailing of provisions constituted the main forms of industrial and commercial activity. The volume of trade passing up and down the Stour was also negligible, though this was offset to some extent by the lively sale of locally produced corn and livestock in the town's weekly market. Indeed, such was

*Cyclists in Church Street, St. Clement*

the slow pace of change that until the 1920s, when a modest amount of house building took place outside of Sandwich, the town as a whole still lay within an area that was bounded by the remains of its medieval walls, ramparts and ditches.

From time to time, however, as in 1914-1918 and 1939-1945, the town was shaken out of its lethargy by the waging of war in Europe. During these stressful years, and especially during the Second World War, the inhabitants of Sandwich were obliged to come to terms with a number of far-reaching changes to their traditional way of life. Indeed, sporadic attacks by enemy aircraft, the arrival of army personnel, the building of gun emplacements, the onset of consumer rationing, the evacuation of children and the arrival of refugees from Europe had an immediate and lasting effect upon the people of Sandwich. The war, therefore, marked an important watershed in the town's history in that it accelerated the pace of its advance into the modern world. This is seen, for example, in the building of a number of private dwellings and a sizeable local authority housing estate on the town's south-western flank during the 1950s, and the appearance of modern consumer goods and services.

**1900**    Sandwich lies so low that only from neighbouring heights can one gain any idea of its general effect, and neighbouring heights are not many. It looks best perhaps from Richborough, next best from the tower of St Clement's Church. As a general rule, when one mounts this latter, one first looks to the south-eastward. One sees the flat marshes, the winding glimmer of the Stour, the purple sea, the unnatural-looking wall of cliffs below the town of Ramsgate. These last throw the whole picture our of composition; give it an unfinished look, as if the artist had forgotten to fill in a parallelogram on his yellowed canvas. At other times they have the immovable, stolid impenetrability, seen above the arm of the sea, of a high-sided ironclad. This view, upon the whole, looks best in a slightly tricky light - when slanting rays of mellowed sunlight pour through towering clouds, when rain impends and the dun of the marshes takes a fresher green...

One revolves a little, sees the hilly land beyond Walmer, great clouds toppling above them; one turns completely - a volte face - and there one is looking at the roofs of some foreign city, some place in a land across the waters where small towns become cities. There is a massing, a clustering of crenellated red roofs - many, many, many. On the flat marshes they seem to rise high in the air. They are very red, very much picked out with tile-shadows. At the tip-top, curiously emphasising the foreign note, stands the tall square tower of St Peter's Church - the tower with the preposterous Dutch bulb at its top. Nothing could be quainter, nothing pleasanter, nothing sweeter, than this assembly of red roofs; nothing more suggestive than that leaden bulb breaking in upon the flat levels of the marsh-land ... one cannot regard it as anything but a Low Country seventeenth-century town.... True, it still has its stock-market. On a Tuesday the droves of bullocks still lose their way in the winding, narrow streets; are still, by the sulphurous voices of the drovers, driven doggedly back into the roads they should follow. But the tone of the place reminds one of Ben Jonson's *Alchemist* ... Sandwich, in fact, is just Bruges, made smaller, sweeter, and more radiant ... Then, again, the sense of orientation of Sandwich seems to be totally undeveloped. The streets of an ordinary English town are moderately crooked; those of Sandwich are warped beyond conception - warped into elbows, into knees, warped till the house-fronts bulge out overhead. One sets out to find something - a church, or an inn at which last year one lodged - but one first finds everything else in the town. Or again, one wishes to make a conscientious tour of the town - to traverse all its streets. One sets out and is for ever running against the doorstep from which one started. It is a looking-glass town, in short. One masters its eccentricities at last, just as did Alice in her case, and one spends pleasant enough hours of exploration. One passes little houses - nearly all the houses are little - whose gardens have trellised gates, affording glimpses of garden mysteries beyond. Their fruit-trees have airs, take the lines of those one sees in the gardens of foreign inns; children peep through the gate-bars as if through convent grilles. Or, through the doorways one sees windows beyond, little square windows with muslin curtains. Little old women stand in the doorways, or by the windows - little old women who ought to be coiffed in white linen. The quaint streets have quaintly fitting names - Delf Street, Knightrider Street, and so on.

There are, however few fine houses in the town - the streets gain their charm from certain gentle humility, from not seeking to overwhelm... The town has one or two showplaces that are worth seeing, but they are somewhat in the way of excrescences. The uniqueness of Sandwich is itself alone. It seems to be a town in hiding - a town that would gladly be forgotten; gladly be left to itself... Thus Sandwich cowers down, hardly visible, amid its marshes; does not flaunt itself on a hill-top as do Rye or Winchelsea... Round about the town go the old earthworks, the former ramparts. Today they form a pleasant promenade for sunny weather, now that the sword of Sandwich has been beaten into a pruning-hook. On a Sunday at sunset they are pleasant to walk upon. If it is near service-time, there is an incredible clangour of bells, which in exalted rivalry outdo each other in outcry of invitation to prayer. There is something golden in the sound - something golden in the red glow of the sunlight on the roofs - something of gold in the old town from which the gold of the earth has passed...The pleasantest view of Sandwich one gets ... is from the ruins of Richborough Castle. These one reaches from the town by taking the street which turns to the left just as the Ramsgate Road makes its exit under the

Barbican Gate. One winds for a time through the devious narrow streets, passes out of them at last into a fair road, then takes an excessively bad one that unostentatiously branches off to the right. One has perhaps a mile and a half of flat, rich ground to cover. The Stour winds sluggishly serpentine through it; a fairly broad, very leisurely piece of water, bordered by bands of rushes and meadow-sweet, and in the summer beloved by cattle, which might stand for a Cuyp of these latter days.

To reach Richborough, one has to climb a little ridge ... One sees St Peter's Church dominating the town, St Clement's tower peeping warily above the house-tops behind; but what draws together the whole picture, the roofs, the Barbican, the bridge, the river, and what not, are the rust-red slants of the few furled barge-sails, the cordage and the vanes of the sparse shipping by the quays. These seem to give a reason to the shining little town, to the gleaming little river, to the flagged marshes, to the sweep of sky. Farther out one sees the sea, between it and the town the great sail of another barge slowly ascending the reaches of the river (J. Hueffer).[71]

**1901** Journeying south we reach Sandwich, once ... one of the most important of English harbours ... [which] wears today the quaint and primitive aspect of an old Flemish city ... The strange - looking tower of St. Peter's ... will ... attract the eye, and it has another two churches of the highest interest. Its town walls have been levelled and made into a pleasant promenade; in its narrow streets there are queer houses, many showing bits of ancient flintwork or whimsical adornment in wood carving; in interiors there are still richly-carved mantlepieces and rare oak panels, laboriously carved ... with grotesque heads; old world gardens peep out from the inclosures of time-worn hospitals. Over them all, in the half-light of a summer evening, floats ... the ringing of the curfew bell (D. Moul and G. Thompson).[72]

**1902** A rattle of cranes and winches sounded from the shipping in the harbour, but the town itself was half asleep. Somnolent shopkeepers in dim back parlours coyly veiled their faces in red handkerchiefs from too ardent flies, while small boys left in charge noticed listlessly the slow passage of time as recorded by the church clock.... The tall grey tower is a landmark at sea, but from the narrow streets of the little town itself it has a disquieting appearance of rising suddenly above the roofs huddled beneath it for the purpose of displaying a black-faced clock with gilt numerals whose mellow chimes here recorded the passing hours for many generations ... the labours of the day were over, and the inhabitants were for the most part out of doors taking the air. Shirt-sleeved householders, leaning against their doorposts smoking, exchanged ideas across the narrow space paved with cobblestones which separated their small and ancient houses, while the

*Strand Street*

matrons, more gregariously inclined, bunched in little groups and discussed subjects which in higher circles would have inundated the land with libel actions ... a street of staid and substantial old houses; houses which had mellowed and blackened with age, but whose quaint windows and chance-opened doors afforded glimpses of comfort attesting to the prosperity of those within. In ... the somewhat squalid streets ... the houses looked dingier than usual; dirty inconvenient little places, most of them with a few cheap gimcracks making a brave show as near the window as possible (W. Jacobs).[73]

**1903** There is so little traffic in the town that grass is said to grow in the streets, although we must confess never to have seen any (W. Dexter).[74]

**c.1904** Sandwich, though no longer enjoying its ancient prestige as a great port, has yet a considerable maritime trade, vessels drawing ten or twelve feet of water being still able to come up the river to the town quay ... It is ... the local capital of an exceedingly fertile and picturesque agricultural district. There is probably no other town in England that has such a quaint old-world air as Sandwich, every stone of which almost appears to speak of past glories, and although the ancient ramparts on the east, west and south of the town have been converted into beautiful promenades, the sloping banks of which are carpeted with green turf, and planted with trees and shrubs, yet there are sufficient remains of ancient architecture to attract the attention of students of archaeology. The town is picturesquely situated on the river Stour as it winds through the marsh before discharging its waters into Pegwell Bay ... The picturesque streets are somewhat irregular according to modern ideas, but they are clean and well-paved, and they contain many architectural features of great interest, including ... many quaint buildings recalling the ... Middle Ages ... St. Bartholomew's Hospital ... a parish almshouse for aged men and women ... St. Clement's Church, a handsome building ... the Parish church of St. Peter, which was built in the early part of the thirteenth century ... It is from the tower of St. Peter's church that the Curfew bell still sends forth its sonorous tones, but, needless to say, the modern inhabitants of Sandwich are not thereby beguiled into spending the remainder of the evening in darkness, or retiring to rest at a particularly early hour.

Richborough Castle, which is but a short distance from the town, is ... the most striking memorial of the Roman occupation of Britain now in existence ... the walls being about twelve feet thick at the base and chiefly built of masses of chalk and large boulders ... Now that the northern wall has been cleared of the ivy which for centuries had almost hidden it from view, it is possible to estimate the former magnificence of the building.

Sandwich has important markets for cattle and corn, and is also the centre of supply for an extensive rural district; so that the town, although its days of commercial supremacy have long since departed, has still very ample trade resources, and contains many capital shops and other business establishments. ...

Sandwich may be a long way behind in many things - is, in fact, a town almost entirely of a past date - but it cannot be said that its inhabitants are one whit less fashionably inclined than their neighbours; and the shops, although they may have an ancient, old-world appearance about their architecture, exhibit the latest novelties in dress and other goods in their windows and showrooms (Deal, Walmer and Sandwich Illustrated).[75]

**1905** The grass grows in the highways of Sandwich, and scarcely a face is seen peeping out of the gabled windows which flank its streets. Except upon a market day, you may look in vain up and down its High Street for a passer-by or a child at play; and indeed it is a common local saying that, in Sandwich, nobody ever goes in or out of the front door of his house except on the occasion of a wedding or a funeral (E. Walford).[76]

**1906** Sandwich is a very staid and grave old town (C. Harper).[77]

**1907** Sandwich, quaint old Cinque Port of tortuous streets and ancient houses... lies on the right bank of the Stour at its extreme southerly bend. As we approach it, the town, dominated by the curiously topped tower of St. Peter's Church, has the look of a foreign city. Over the river is a toll bridge and a quaint (restored) barbican spans the road... North, Sandwich looks over the flats by ancient Stonar and more ancient Richborough to Ebbsfleet and Thanet; east it looks over sandy levels to where the retreating sea has gone, and all about these level river and shore meadows is now played the royal and ancient game of golf ..

It is said to be a good test of a man's bump of locality if once having visited Sandwich he can find his way through it - say from the Canterbury to the Deal roads - without making a misturning. The thing has been done. Dotted about the town are old houses of Tudor and earlier times ... Bits of carved decoration and old doorways and windows are to be seen in many of the streets ... Once the most famous port in the Kingdom ... is said only to have "wakened up" during the past quarter of a century or so since the great golf revival (W. Jerrold).[78]

**1907** Sandwich lies among the marshes left by the sea on its retirement from the bluffs of Richborough and Minster ... From horizon to horizon there is no single elevation to cast a shadow or to intercept the sunshine. Only when clouds are riding and sea winds sweeping over, are the bright colours of the town and its gleaming belt of meadow and river obscured ... Since the harbour silted up ... its bye-gone importance and wealth are attested by the remains that give it a picturesqueness such as few places can rival. it is even now largely a survival of the Middle Ages. Looking at some of its streets to-day, we can see how English towns looked in the time of the Tudors ...

Sandwich is one of the few towns where the old-time ramparts stand. As grassy mounds, they girdle the town - except where the waters of the Haven wash the quays and wharves. At places the old masonry crops out, refusing to be hidden, and where the main roads leave the town the stone foundations of the vanished gateways are exposed. From these ramparts it is possible to see the fine and varied groupings of the huddled red roofs, above which rise the mighty square tower of St. Clement's and the bulbous top of St. Peter's. Without the ramparts there are very few houses.

Within the town, its history is attested by a hundred facts. You may note the tortuous maze of narrow, winding streets, the ancient and differing houses. Into the construction of houses is worked much old masonry. In walls, gables, and angles there are square blocks of stone, masses of rubble, flints raggedly set or regularly squared and faced, oddments of carving, the dripstone or tympanum of a door, the moulding of an arch, a boss or a corbel, indifferently and inconsequently worked in. Fine pieces of wood-carving are used as door lintels. To see the houses in their most picturesque aspect you must view them from the back of an alley, where tier upon tier of gables, wings and projections, tower one above another, or from the tower of St. Peter's, when the medly of warm red roofs effectually conceals the twisting lines of the streets. The very names of the streets strike a medieval note, and the music of sweet bells floats on the still air.

There are comparatively few gardens. The town of medieval days was too much compressed for gardens. But the Delf - an artificial water channel made in the days of Edward I - wanders through the streets, running between stone walls and under tiny bridges (in the crevices of which are harts-tongue ferns, wallflowers and snapdragons), in front of the house doors. There are massive oak doors, curious knockers, and old insurance plates. The churchyards are full of graves with carved headstones; in the churches are the tombs and monuments of the great merchants and traders of the flourishing days.

There are fine old houses, large and beautiful. Two of these were built in the year of Shakespeare's birth. Others are even older, but at about that time there were clearly able craftsmen working in the town. There are the carvings in the Town Hall; the carved supports of the projecting upper storey of the King's Arms, in Strand Street; a carved lintel over Three Kings' Yard; beautiful plaster ceilings; oak panelling; and other pieces of work all showing what skilled artificers were in Sandwich in Elizabeth's days.

Then, too, there are the public buildings. Oldest of these are the three churches, St. Clement's, St. Mary's, and St. Peter's, with the chapel of St. Bartholomew's Hospital, each with distinctive points of interest, all telling of early prosperity. There are the gates, Fisher's Gate and the Barbican, reminding one of walled defences, and telling of the insecurity of the Middle Ages, when ravage and massacre were everyday dangers. And there is the Town Hall, reflecting the solid comfort and well-being that in Tudor days had not yet passed from the town as a consequence of the destruction of the harbour.

That all these buildings were founded is tangible witness to a past of prosperity, not perhaps wholly unbroken, yet so continuous that successive centuries marked accretion and development. On the other hand, that so much of the medieval should remain so little altered, that the walls should not have been encroached upon, that the narrow, winding streets are even now as they were planned - these things tell just as clearly of a limit to prosperity, an end of growth ... The key to the rise and fall of Sandwich is found in the withdrawal of the sea ...

In a tranquillity rarely disturbed, the little town rests, lighted by the glory of its past, proud of its ancient fame, jealous of its hoary relics. Its story lives in books ... lives in stones and masonry which may be seen now much .as they were a century, two centuries, even three and four centuries ago. So when we leave the little town we shall cherish the memory of its quaint streets; of the derelict city of Stonar across the bridge ... of the Dutch scene ... where St. Bartholomew's stands. The grass edged open road, the few poplars that quiver in a dancing reflection in the narrow dyke, the spire of the tiny church at Worth, the endless distances of the unbroken marshes - these are typically Dutch. They will linger in the memory as do the pictures of Dutch masters ...

To the present day visitor the quiet, restful little town, with its picturesquely clustered roofs and quaint towers, its beauty of grouping and outline, its exquisite colouring and general air of peaceful calm; seems to be "a place of memories," a town whose busy life is closing amid an aureole of warlike memories and peaceful benedictions. Standing at sunset on the Mill Wall, with the town sinking into the shadows of night behind one; in front the railway station, its twinkling lights and the floating smoke of an incoming train furnishing a striking note of contrast between the historic town and the more modern life beyond its borders, one cannot fail to be impressed by the calm beauty of the scene. Then, as one turns to gaze across the old town, gradually becoming more indistinct as the shadows lengthen and the night follows hard upon the declining day ... One can see the ships riding safely in the Haven, and over all a sense of prosperity and leisurely activity.

At the time of writing Sandwich is experiencing another of those waves of prosperity which have formed so curious a feature of its history, showing the tenacity with which the old town clings to its life. This new prosperity is due to two main causes, first, the modern desire for recreation by the seaside and the national love of pastime, and, secondly, the increased haven tariff caused by the conveyance of materials to Dover, for the new Dover Harbour.

The modern desire for recreation has been taken advantage of by the public-spirited action of the present Earl of Guilford, who has opened up his estate at the seaside. Here a light railway has been constructed, which affords means of conveyance for building materials, etc., in various directions to the building sites. Several residential buildings, as that of Sir John Dixon Poynder, are good specimens of the class of residence most favoured in the new scheme. In addition to this, the enterprise of the town authorities is shown in the wisely-planned improvements which are constantly being carried out. It is probably correct to say that more buildings have been recently erected in or near Sandwich than at any time during the last hundred years, The opening up of the Guilford estate, where a splendid hotel has been built and numerous roads cut, together with its proximity to Sandwich station and from thence its easily attained access to London, must very shortly render Sandwich a most eligible and pleasant health resort.

It is only fair to say that the first impetus in this direction was given by the establishment a few years ago, of the Royal St. George's golf club, the English "St. Andrew's," which, by its twin merits of excellence of situation and suitability for the game, as also its easy accessibility from London, gave to the London golfer the first reasonably accessible course of a first-class nature in England, and created what may be termed an epoch in the history of English golf. So great has been the success of this club that during the present year a new club, "The Prince's," has been opened, under the distinguished captaincy of the Right Hon. A.J. Balfour.

*Poulterer's shop, Fisher Street in the late nineteenth century*

The increased haven traffic has brought to the exchequer of the town a corresponding increase in haven dues, which has converted the heavy deficit of recent years into a balance in hand amounting to several thousands of pounds. It seems evident, therefore, that the future of Sandwich is to be viewed with the very hopeful belief that its long period of insignificance, poverty, and neglect is now at an end ...

Among the industries of Sandwich in the early nineteenth century was numbered that of ship-building. This, like others which might be enumerated, has gradually declined, and for the last decade has been practically non-existent. In its place, however, there have arisen two others, the manufacture of parchment and the packing of fish and fruit. In connection with the latter it is a remarkable coincidence that the nation which in early days was so inveterate an enemy, and was so largely responsible for the sacking, burning and assault of the town, is in this year of grace supplying workmen to assist in its return to prosperity. Every year at the packing season Frenchmen are brought into Sandwich to assist in the fish and fruit packing.

Until quite recently the principal, if not the only interest which Sandwich possessed for outside people was the antiquarian interest. Of this it has enough and to spare. Its clustering red roofs and quaint towers, its tortuous and cobble paved streets, its mysterious courts and alley-ways, flanked and darkened by the overhanging upper stories of its quaint old houses, speak eloquently of the days of Elizabeth and the Stuarts, and of the still earlier days of the Norman and the Saxon ... all these things rise before us as we pace the half-deserted streets of the dozing town, which is just now beginning once more to shake off its lethargy and adapt itself to the newer civilisation and strenuous life of modern times (G. Gray).[79]

**1907**    Sandwich is a market town ... and is on the River Stour, in the midst of a wide area of rich marsh land, through which the river winds its circuitous course to Pegwell Bay and the sea, here distant from the town about 2 miles at the nearest point ... The streets are narrow and irregularly built, but are paved and lighted; the ancient walls which surrounded the town on the east, west and south side have been razed and sloping banks formed, covered with grass and planted with shrubs, and the summit of the embankment forms a promenade... The Curfew Bell is still rung here morning and evening...A corn market is held every Wednesday from 2 to 4 p.m. at the Fleur-de-Lis, and an extensive cattle market every alternate Monday from 8 to 12 a.m.

The trade of the town consists chiefly in tanning and wool-sorting, and the importation of coal, timber and stone and the export of corn, malt, hops, fruit and wool. There is a brewery, malting-houses, iron foundry and tannery. The importation of coal for the supply of the large agricultural district around is very extensive (Kelly's Directory).[80]

**1907** A short walk brings us to ... the highroad from Ramsgate to Sandwich ... the wind blows keenly across the stretches of desolate marsh-lands; clouds sail over head, their shadows coursing across the green sward; away to the left is the long sea-wall guarding the lowlands, the mouth of the meandering Stour ... and glimpses of ships upon the sea ... So on along the dusty road ... until we come opposite Richborough ... the towering, mossy, frowning wall of the ancient fortress ... How changed the view now from what it was then; silence now in place of the tramp of armed men; cattle grazing and ploughed fields where the sea glittered in the sunshine or turned to grey beneath the lowering storm clouds; only these stern fragments remaining of the strong fort, draped with greenery, sheep stolidly browsing in their midst.

Sandwich - the village on the sands - is a picturesque relic of glorious days, when the sea came up to her quays and her ships were ever forward in the fray ... As a port, the history of Sandwich makes great and sad reading, great in the far past, sad in the latter years ... few sounds of life come to our ears ... Richborough broods upon its hill ... the Stour flows slowly past, on its nine-mile journey to the sea; there are the green banks, the sails of barges, the lush meadows, the cattle - a Dutch picture ... With a sigh over what has been, we walk ... alongside the river ... to the bridge, where we will join the loafers who ever frequent it. Turning our backs ... we face the Tudor Barbican, a suitably picturesque entry to the picturesque town ... Let us enter in, and turn to our right down Strand Street, with it quaint, beetling houses ... The atmosphere of Sandwich is against vigorous exercise; you can stroll through its old streets, but not walk. One way and another there is much to see ... narrow winding streets, dark lanes, half-timbered housefronts, carved doorways ... and delightful Saint Clement's Church, whose tower is the most conspicuous feature of the town, impressive and dignified as are all towers of Norman work (W. Shore).[81]

**1910** Sandwich ... a whole town, complete, perfect ... an unparalleled exemplar of the old England that has passed away... the winding narrow streets, old rights of way built in on to the furthermost inch; the overhanging storeys that shut out the sky, so that underneath them one might almost be walking in a tunnel; the exaltation of the old churches over all; the market square and Town Hall; the road-side watercourses; the little enclosed meadows;

the garden houses, and walled residences of the gentry and well-to-do; the town gates; all these, bound in by the round of the old ramparts, and supplemented on one side by the river winding to the sea, give a presentation that is unique in modern England (Pike's Blue Book).[82]

**1910** One's first impression of Sandwich is that it gets its full value out of its bells, tuneful bells doubtless, but seemingly over busy. What with chiming the quarters and striking the hours, and the whole eight of them pealing for services and weddings and rejoicings and practisings, and the tenor going every morning at five as "the rising bell," and at eight o'clock every evening as "the curfew bell," and whenever a native or inhabitant dies, so many strokes for so many years and as many again at the funeral... they never seem to be at rest.

The cattle market seems to be going as strong as at any time during the seven hundred years or more it has been in existence. Sheep, oxen, cows, pigs, horses, and no side shows: farmers' traps fifty in a row by the Fleur de Lys, and others elsewhere, the horses out of all of them put up somewhere thereabouts: the whole Market Place is alive, and sometimes every pen full. Sandwich is not so sleepy as it is said to be, and certainly it does not sleep around its Town Hall on market day (W. Gordon).[83]

**1911** The old-world town of Sandwich has many points of attraction ... Situated on low-lying flat land, only reclaimed from the sea within historic times, it can rightly be considered as a coast town, although with the silting up of its haven its possibilities as a port have well-nigh vanished ... it is notable as an example of a medieval town still almost entirely within the limits of its ancient walls. Raised ramparts trace the position of the old walls almost all round the town ... The aspect of the town, as seen across the surrounding flats, is almost more Dutch or Flemish than English, and its quaint, crooked streets, bristling with examples of old-time architecture, carry us back to Tudor times. The town shows clear evidences of past prosperity and has distinct indications of the departure of that greatness (J. Roget).[84]

**1911** The red walls of Sandwich, with the little bulbous leaden spire that surmounts the brick tower of St. Peter's, and forms one of those unarchitectural but picturesque features ... dominate the marshy scene as you proceed towards Deal. Sandwich, once a great port, now stands quite dry and inland, but no one, I suppose, would walk along the coast without visiting it. Many a sketch has been made of its Barbican Gate - the bridge ending with a red arch that stands on chequered supports of grey and brown, the glinting waters, the flat foreground before the river, the quaint top-forward houses, the masts on the Stour, and the flowers and trees of gardens coming up to walls on the river-brink ... The streets in general, with houses of two or three stories, and the higher stories projecting over the lower ones, with fronts showing timber rafters and pink or brown plaster, and with red-tiled roofs which lichen has spotted with green ... the whole town has a visible, tangible character that makes it agreeable to loaf in. The old market-place, the walk on the Butts, where the city walls once were, a walk with houses and gardens on one side and the open marshes with elms, fences, cows, houses, and masts dotted for an indefinite distance on the open flatness, on the other ... (A. Lewis).[85]

**1913** Sandwich ... a town which is largely petrified, so to speak, the very form and mould of the town of earlier centuries. It is as to a place picturesque, historical, romantic, that visitors come to Sandwich. There is plenty for them to see in the little town that dreams on the marshes, surrounded to this day by the embankments and the moats of its old town walls. There are three fine churches ... beautiful old houses ... every street in Sandwich is full of interest ... and from its situation it is blessed with an exhilarating air, and inspires a great sense of openness and freedom. . (P. Row).[86]

**1914** Approaching Sandwich, whose towers and roof tops rise picturesquely ahead from the level marshes, mingled with the masts and spars of a few vessels lying at the town quays, a belt of spindly trees is passed, stretching away to the left. They are trees of a considerable height and size, but they wear an ill-nourished appearance ... The ancient town ... is entered by a bridge across the Stour ... Against its parapets lean the idle, the born tired, and the infirm of Sandwich the livelong day; some staring into the water, or vaguely across the sandy flats; others facing north, expending a fascinated stare upon the activities of the brewery, which is the busiest thing in the town. There are more imposing entrances than this to English towns ... but no other approach is so truly quaint as that to Sandwich by the Barbican. Little, squatty-round towers with their lower half chequered black and white in flint and stone, and their upper part finished with peaked roofs like witches' hats, give an effect almost unreal in their completely picturesque setting, with the curious tower of St. Peter's peering over the roof tops ... Today the size and shape of the town are what they always were. The ramparts still look out upon the open, level meadows ... and so it has drowsed away the last centuries, ... So much has been said of Sandwich as a 'dead town' that strangers who first come to it full of the tales they have heard, of grass growing in the streets - and, for all I know, moss growing on its inhabitants - are likely to be surprised at its comparative vitality. Grass does not grow like a lawn in the streets of Sandwich, in spite of all the far-fetched stories of decay and desolation ... and it is something of a shock to find a quite busy railway station just outside the ramparts and a very modern 'Stores' in whose windows are all sorts of twentieth-century provisions, for which modern coin of the realm ... must be tendered. All these signs, including the occasional motor-cars that hurry through the narrow streets, are very reassuring, or very disastrous, according to your point of view.

At Sandwich, which is supposed ... to have given up the ghost long ago, but has done nothing of the kind, there should certainly be no railway, and there should be no room in a 'dead' town for the gasworks which may be seen - and smelt - on the quay, nor for the particularly large and busy brewery in Strand Street ... If one really wishes to see a dead town, Winchelsea or New Romney ... may be recommended. They are much more dead ... than Sandwich.

There is no grand architecture, of the wonder-compelling kind, in Sandwich. It is all very quiet and modest and domestic, but at the same time old-world and reverend. Of the three parish churches, St. Clement's ... is the most notable and has a fine Norman tower ... St. Peter's is perhaps better known, because its tower is taller and is capped with a curious Dutch-like turret, and rising to a considerable height, viewed from a distance, across the flats, it is the most prominent feature of the town. The tower is frankly and unashamedly unarchitectural ... But it is to be hoped that the modern passion for remodelling plain buildings and putting them into a conventional dress will pass this tower of St. Peter's by; for Sandwich would scarce seem the same Sandwich without it, and people who write about the town would lose the cherished chance of being mildly funny at its expense.

I do not think any stranger has ever been known to find his way through Sandwich without making one or two false turns, for its streets are winding and deceptive. The house of the Middle Ages is not represented in them at all, and it is a sixteenth and seventeenth-century Sandwich you see, not the medieval port. It is, in general, a Dutch effect, as if those settlers ... had imported their views upon domestic architecture and had successfully imposed them upon the town.

There is now a stir in the old streets of Sandwich ... Recently the trustees of the Earl of Guilford have constructed a 'private' road from Sandwich, across the sandy wastes, to the sea, where they have erected a smart hotel, chiefly for golfers, on what was the solitary shore. Sometimes, when the golfers have bored each other almost to extinction with bragging of their remarkable feats on the course, they lounge into Sandwich and patronise it. To those who do not play golf all these developments are hateful and infuriating ... Meanwhile the boys and growing lads of Sandwich employed as caddies are being bred up to be idle, vicious and unemployable men (C. Harper).[87]

**1917** The way between Canterbury and Sandwich runs in an almost direct line; it is the Roman road from Richborough... The road, like many in Kent, is switchback; it is not crowded with traffic, albeit the motor is not infrequent. There are pleasant hop-fields and green lands, a very wealth of old houses, some charming churches and an occasional windmill.

A little way farther on and I entered the green level plain which lines the coast. The country had quite a Dutch look and in the distance were the towers of Sandwich; ditches took the place of canals; there was a sprinkling of windmills. The Flemish refugees who fled from Alva's persecution in the Low Countries must have found themselves quite at home in Sandwich. They, in their turn, made their mark. The bulbous tower of St. Peter's Church, bits of house architecture, even some words peculiar to the district, all remind of the Netherlands. ... As the day wore on I was soon wandering in the narrow streets of Sandwich. A curious and intricate jumble, they form for the stranger a sort of maze of town architecture difficult to unravel until experience gives the key. You are continually missing the point at which you aim, continually passing the same spot, yet the space enclosed by the ramparts is comparatively small, for a brisk walk of twenty minutes would I think take you completely round it. Do not regret the lost way; in every corner there is some little bit of old-world architecture delightful to your sight. It were worth coming to Sandwich merely to see a beautiful house like Manwood Court, where was once the grammar School which is now housed in more spacious quarters outside the ramparts. Those ramparts have done much to preserve the antique aspect of the place. Of late years golf has given it a new prosperity, and there are many new houses, but these have been erected in the new suburbs, outside or away beyond the golf links, by the sea, and so do not mar the past... I went along the High Street and out at the Barbican, that quaint medieval passage or gate ... and walked about a little in the Haven. It is not quite deserted, for, when the tide fills, one or two barges rise lazily from the mud and crawl past the bridge, and out into the marsh, after which they are tugged, or perhaps if the wind be favourable, sail towards the main. There are some fragments of the Town Wall hereabouts which you easily pick out ... There is, still, a small fragment left of the Sandown Gate. As the name implies it leads to the downs and the sea. It ought to be called Golf Course Gate. On this Saturday afternoon all sorts of vehicles were streaming through it on their way to the Course, and I went there too. There was some important match on, so the place was crowded. The local constabulary were hard pressed to give order and regularity to the traffic. It was a full mile distant from the town over the downs, or perhaps one should say links ... I went on an additional mile to the sea, where the houses of a new Sandwich are springing up, huge and "replete with every comfort," no doubt, yet monstrous, hideous, formless, as if the architects had taken for plan the distorted visions of a rich man's nightmare, such be the strange growths that the last few years have raised on this once lonely shore.

On Sunday morning I ... sought a seat on the Mill Wall; it was under the shadow of St. Clement's, the chief church of the place. The exquisite Norman tower with its quaint arcades stood out perfectly outlined in the clear air, from it there pealed forth the sweet note of its melodious bells. Past it motors hooting loudly, as they dashed round the street corners, sped at a mad pace and in quick succession through the Sandown Gate on towards the links. Through the trees I saw the masts and sails of a barge slowly moving from the haven. The bells seemed the plaintive, pathetic note of old-world faith calling in vain to men intent on pelf or pleasure. Presently the bells of St. Peter's and St. Mary's echoed from the near distance in a confused, sweet jumble of sound. With such music in my ears, I loitered for some time in the Rope Walk, and then after a final glance at the old houses of Strand Street, set my face towards ... Canterbury (F. Watt).[88]

**1921**  Sandwich lies upon the flat ... It also lies within its ancient bounds, having strayed at scarcely any point beyond its original ramparts, which, still plain for all to see, circumvent it. It has not as yet any meanly-built suburbs or tentacles, disfiguring its outskirts... Green meadows still spread and lush orchards still wave up to the very lines where its defenders stood of old to beat back, should fate permit of it, the attacking Dane or Frenchman. A few sumptuous residences to be sure, standing in leafy grounds, have been built of late without the walls on the seaward side, but they scarcely at all disturb the ancient peace of the atmosphere. That new Richborough has not so disturbed it would be saying too much. Still its temporary outskirts are a good half-mile away, and whatever its future may be, if it has any, the worst from this point of view is over, and its business centre is thrice that distance off and may be abnormally active without seriously contaminating Sandwich. The population of the town is about 3,000. The Stour washes its walls and a few boats of light draft have hitherto been accustomed to find their way up the muddy but now much transformed river. It is also a market town and, as all the world knows, a golfing centre, its two deservedly famous courses trailing over and around the sand-dunes which border the sea two miles away. But apart from a hotel or two and some private residences outside the walls and more numerous buildings on the distant shore, I don't think Sandwich town does a great deal of entertaining, other than day-visitors, who come to wander vaguely about its quaint tortuous streets for an hour or two and generally to lose their way several times in the process.

For I do not know any little town whose streets meander so inconsequently, or whose geography is so baffling. Till you have developed some further acquaintance with it, you are almost certain, while endeavouring to reach a particular point within the town, to find yourself brought up short on the ramparts, in the open country, or by the river, or quite possibly at the very spot from whence you started! This does not greatly matter, since the town is as small as its throughfares are, to the stranger at least, disconcerting. Each of them seems to pursue its own independent and winding way, following no doubt the trail to which local exigencies or surface obstacles compelled the feet of its burghers hundreds of years ago.

If they strike other streets, equally absent-minded, at any angle it seems to be rather by accident than design. All this, however, adds no little to that air of picturesque antiquity which Sandwich maintains from one end to the other. For nearly all the houses in all the streets are old. Early Georgian, to be sure, is the prevailing type, as for many and obvious reasons must be the case in all our oldest towns, though who shall say how many ancient structures lurk behind a Georgian fronts But among these mellow brick fronts there are still to be seen unaltered great numbers of half-timbered Tudor and Jacobean buildings, many of them with projecting upper storeys.

There is only one main gateway standing, and that is where the town is entered by a bridge across the river carrying the road from Thanet. This is known as the Barbican and provides the most fitting entrance to the town for a visitor who proposes to soak himself for a while in its ancient spirit. It is not, however, medieval but Tudor, the original gates having all, unhappily, vanished ... But one medieval gate does in fact remain to Sandwich. It opens out of the old wall on to the little used wharves, which here line the river and is known as Fisher's Gate, its two-storied gatehouse over the pointed arch being lighted by thirteenth century double-light lancet windows. This other Barbican gate, however, timber-capped and with two timber-capped drum towers, opens into the High Street, which, characteristically edging away from the busier part of the town, leads nowhere particular and does apparently no business of its own worth mentioning. It mainly consists of quiet and rather humble old dwellings with the exception of a fine old panelled Tudor house faced in Georgian style and with flint which serves unofficially as the Rectory to St. Clements. Some of the Sandwich streets run extraordinarily brief careers. Chain Street, for instance, in which High Street casually terminated, is just twenty-two yards long - hence its name...

Nearly the whole town is tile-roofed and ... there are to be had from many points whole vistas of such roofs, mellow in tint and quaintly curved and sagged by time, with chimney stacks to match in date and wholly sympathetic in pose. A few old houses, for their size and importance, stand out about the rest, such, for instance, as that one, now known as Manwood Court, at the north edge of the town which shows up well, being isolated in its own grounds ...

The nomenclature of the streets and quarters in Sandwich is all that it should be. There is Bowling Street, Knightrider Street, Harnet Street, and Delf Street, the last-named from a stream which six centuries ago some Dutch engineers brought into the town from distant springs as a water supply and which served that purpose till almost the other day. Then there is Loop Street, King Street, Fisher Street, Moat Sole, The Butts, The Beagrams and other such suggestive designations.

Short bits of the old wall survive inconspicuously here and there, but all along the west side of the town the old ramparts have been fashioned into a delightful promenade, such as may be found in so many old continental cities. Here you may make the circuit of nearly half the town and, raised well above it, enjoy many charming inward glimpses of old-fashioned gardens and orchards, breaking with their verdant patches of lawn, leaf and blossom, the irregular lines of red gabled roof. The rampart slopes are neatly turfed and in some sections gay with shrubs and flower beds, in others shaded by avenues of trees. A narrow waterway now fills what was once the ditch or moat beneath them, and beyond all is orchard or open meadow. Altogether Sandwich maintains its ancient character with cleanliness, good taste and self-respect, and apparently without any conscious effort. It is all or almost all good to look upon. There are many houses whose years would seem almost too great to be borne, but there are no depressing slums . Of frequent occurrence too are early Georgian doorcaps, Flemish gables and queer little windows which seem as if they had escaped the notice of later builders and restorers. Let us hope the local authorities will be wise in their generation and treat this historic little town with tender hand. There is only one Sandwich in England ...

The road from Sandwich to the sea crosses the old moat, which just here does duty as a Bowling Green, at the site of the old Sandown gate, and after

*Durrant's grocer's shop in Strand Street*

a mile or so through enclosed fields, with a sumptuous villa set here and there beside it; breaks out on to the open dunes and Golf Links of the St. George's Club. The old farmhouse, among its grove of trees which constitutes the present club-house, lies picturesquely to the left, alone breaking the wide expanse of green turf and sandhill which sweeps away eastward to the sea front. Along this, however, where the road from Sandwich debouches on the shore is a whole settlement of private villas on which architects in the palmy pre-war days have obviously expended no little care and ingenuity, and a good deal of taste. This is a great deal more than can be said for the hotel, a rectangular erection of dreary grey masonry soaring heavenward in defiant and unabashed ugliness to an unconscionable height. Upon this graceful sweep of sandy beach, which in bright summer days trails its golden belt between the blue sea and the verdant hinterland, from the Stour mouth to Deal, this monstrous edifice constitutes a truly hideous blot. Whether from the Ramsgate cliffs on the north, from the Kingsdown heights above Walmer, to the southward, or from miles away on far inland ridges, this unsightly pile dominates the whole shoreline and mars the harmony of a noble prospect to an extent that has only to be seen to be realized. Comfort and convenience could surely have been secured at less outrage to the natural amenities of Sandwich Bay (A. Bradley).[89]

**1924** ... Sandwich ... is in a sense the successor of Richborough, whose massive grey walls, planted nearly two thousand years ago on this uplifted plateau above the Stour, are within easy sight of it. ... Lifted high above the Stour marshlands, it hits you in the eye miles away, this 600 yards or so of massive wall some thirty feet high and forming three sides of a vast square ... rising, as it were, inconsequently amid pastures and grain fields. This very aloofness, indeed, seems to enhance its mystery. ...

Today ... [Sandwich] is two miles from the sea with a river connexion not worth considering ... Drained marshlands, rich in produce and in pasture, surround it upon all sides, merging seaward into sandy commons and ridgy dunes where the famous golf links ... reach out their furthest tentacles to those of Deal ...

Today an occasional sailing barge comes up the Stour to dump some coal or timber on an absent-minded looking wharf ... The present-day appeal of Sandwich reserves itself till the visitor has crossed the bridge over the Stour, which washes one side of the town, and passed under a Barbican gateway of Tudor origin. For from the flats around, save for its three upstanding old church towers, little is visible but a line of rooftops and red-tiled gables; broken here and there by foliage. The town still squats compactly within the lines and remains of its old defences, while its modern extensions are negligible. The twisting streets and by-ways still follow wayward courses ... In Sandwich these seem to the visitor delightfully inconsequent. In a first cursory ramble, with a general aim of achieving the farther limits of the little town, he will almost certainly find himself before very long at the point he started from. It almost suggests the Maze at Hampton Court! This confusion may be in part accounted for by the constant attraction on one side or the other of quaint old houses, beguiling one up some twisting side street or court which in its turn opens out further and fresh gems of Tudor or Jacobean work, till one's bearings are utterly lost. This matters, of course, less than nothing, for it is the general atmosphere of the old town, not a few outstanding antiquities, that makes for its charm and interest, and it is just the place for loitering about inconsequently ...

I know no little English town which in its domestic architecture from one end to the other gives a more abiding impression of the past, and shows a greater number of Tudor and Jacobean houses along its winding street fronts. They are mostly of timber, many with overhanging upper storeys, and are none the less effective for serving sometimes as modest shops and humble dwellings or taverns in a clean, self-respecting, matter-of-course fashion; for nothing approaching a factory disturbs the ancient peace of Sandwich. It slumbers in a profound repose, almost uncanny with so many near neighbours to the north and south rather more than wide-awake! In truth, this serene atmosphere adds immensely to its aesthetic qualities. It has no slums, though it contains nearly 3,000 souls who must exist mainly by serving the needs of an agricultural district ...

Not the least attractive feature of the place is the fashion in which the old ramparts have been laid out in broad terraces, with grassy banks and flower-beds, here and there bordered with shady trees. With orchards and green pasture on the one hand, the town lies on the other at a rather lower elevation displaying a most felicitous prospect of red-tile roofs mingled with the verdure of leafy gardens (Cornhill Magazine).[90]

**1925**   There are two towns and many villages in the Region which in addition to their historic importance are in actual possession of remains on a sufficient scale to make them beautiful as well as interesting, and that to a degree rarely surpassed in this country. There is danger that these historic beauties are not always fully appreciated in a district which has passed through the industrial revolution of the last century without scathe ... Canterbury and Sandwich have perhaps been taken for granted by many of the inhabitants of East Kent, and their antique features, which do not fit in with modern requirements, even regarded as drawbacks. Before an insidious change is wrought by industrialization, it is necessary to proclaim the importance of these places, not only to a few artists and admirers of old buildings but as representing one of the most valuable assets of the community... If Canterbury exhibits the problem of a city whose complex vitality has never flagged, Sandwich is a simpler and perhaps a rarer case. The scale of the two places is remarkably different: Canterbury has something of Roman directness about its main streets ... Sandwich is medievalism on its most intimate and homely scale. Unlike those rectangular towns, Winchelsea, Flint and the French Bastides, ... Sandwich is a maze of curved lines, the logic of whose arrangement is unrevealed to the modern eye ... it has a richness of interest and copiousness of authentic vestiges of antiquity which remind one of the cities of Flanders, France, Italy or Bavaria - enhanced perhaps for us by a distinctive flavour of Flemish influence in its buildings. The town plan is as precious as its series of street pictures (P. Abercrombie).[91]

**1926**   This must be a genuine saunter through Sandwich - just a stroll. It would be cruel to hurry, equally impossible to linger. And for the same reason - this old-world spot in Kent, and the most unique in England, is so full of relics that the act of walking quickly cheats you of great pleasure, and if you stay long to look at all the old buildings you cannot finish your walk in a day.

The fame of so many old-world towns rests upon past glories only, but here, at Sandwich, rich though it be in historic associations, tangible treasures remain. There is no doubt about the age of the place - age in its timbered houses, which, sheltering each other, have withstood the ravages of weather. Many are to be found just as they were built, others disfigured by the encasement of overhangs; some have modern fronts; and there are even modern shops.

Yet, somehow, the streets - narrow streets, many of them with windows on one side looking straight into windows on the other - never lose their characteristics. You seem to breathe an atmosphere connected directly with the past, a halo of antiquity hangs overhead and you almost expect to scent the fustiness of an unwashed town - that musty air that issues from unventilated attics and dark, disused passages. But no. Sandwich may have narrow streets and many of them, the inhabitants may be clustered closely together, but there is no suggestion of uncleanliness. Everything is trim - well-groomed - from public building to private dwelling. And there are no slums - many passages, but no slums.

The only complaint that the average visitor makes is that although it may be easy to get into the town it's very difficult to find his way out. He traverses a street which apparently takes him to the Canterbury road, but it's odds against him reaching the desired goal. He twists and turns and finds himself back in the place from whence he started. He makes another attempt - with the same result. He has lost his bearings utterly, but so courteous and accustomed to help the lost traveller are the people of Sandwich that they willingly send him off again on the right track. And - once more - well, we'll leave it at that. These good Sandwichians love you so much that they must have laid out their town in the form of a maze to keep you inside for all time (C. Igglesden).[92]

**1936** Not quite of our Motherland is the surprising town of Sandwich. It stands alone, a child of the past that refuses to grow with the centuries. It has lost the sea ... It has lost its great importance as a port. But the mysterious spirit of the past has refused to die in these queer winding streets, in these ancient houses and the quaint ways that lead to them ... Indoors and outdoors Sandwich is remarkable ... The hours go by ... and we do not tire, for there is much to keep us everywhere ... for its winding streets, its houses, the atmosphere of long ago that will not leave it, are a continual delight (A. Mee).[93]

**1940** We will return to the coast across the country direct to Sandwich ... As we leave the North Downs behind us, there occurs a conspicuous change in the countryside; it seems that ... England has become suddenly bored with being English: this extreme corner has the character, or rather lack of character, of the Netherlands. And to emphasise the change we even find houses from beyond the North Sea - seventeenth century houses left by Flemish refugees from the Spanish wars; there are villages near Sandwich whose streets might have been painted by Pieter de Hoogh. ... The town's position today is curious; refugees we still see - no longer Flemish, but Czech... as yet they do no more than wander through the narrow sleepy streets uncertain whether to be grateful for their escape from a concentration camp or bored to tears. Not that Sandwich of today needs assistance ... The famous St. George's Club is the most irritating golf course in all England, and therefore, so it seems, the best. Today, tournaments and tourists keep picturesque Sandwich thriving (R. Wyndham).[94]

**1946** My first impression was that it was far larger than I expected it to be. My second was that it was not only foreign, but medievally foreign. It has a Dutch look about it. Its streets are many, extremely narrow, crowded with houses of extra-ordinary variety in style of building, with many steep pitched red roofs. In the midst, above the huddled roofs rose a magnificent church tower. The compact little town is compressed within a grassy rampart similar to that which surrounds Wareham ... I find it hard to restrain my language about Sandwich, but the reason for my enthusiasm is no doubt in part due to the treatment that I received at the Bell. I tested the quality of the beer in 29 of its 30 pubs only to find that the bar of the Bell was far the cosiest, the beer the best. I visited the market and was disappointed ... The crowd was greatest round not sheep but a bicycle which went for 17s. 6d. The enthusiasm was most marked for a decayed-looking lorry. There were also harmonicas and shot-guns being auctioned. The trippers from Margate and Ramsgate who had come over by bus were thrilled by the quaintness of the scene. I was more astonished by the quaintness of their clothes,... The women sightseers wore thin summer frocks, nylon stockings and white tennis shoes. The wisest virgins carried or wore diaphanous mackintoshes of crude scarlet, more prophylactic than prophylactery ... It is quite a place to get lost in. I never got the hang of those narrow streets and twittens ... As I wandered round the grassy ramparts above the dry outer ditch I looked out on the Gallows Field and the Guestling Stream. They had lost some of their terror, for a merry-go-round was raucous on the former and small urchins were searching for tiddlers in the latter. I passed the Butts where the men of Sandwich practised the archery that helped to bring victory at Creçy and Agincourt. I looked down from Mill Wall to the smoothest lawn I have ever seen, where the city fathers forget our modern discontents in practising the ancient game of bowls.... We saw the ancient Delf Stream which until 40 years ago supplied the town with water and still follows a course of its own under pavements and houses ... We drove on to the Prince's golf course, and found the windows of the club house all shattered, paint peeling off and a general air of decay. Black-out curtains still flapped in the wind. It was a depressing sight... There seems to my mind no reason to keep up the pretence that the Stour was any good to Sandwich. First the sea deserted her and then the river. But Sandwich has no cause for regret. She has had a grand history and there's still market- gardening, there's still golf, there's still a very good type of resident. Sandwich is flourishing (S. Mais).[95]

**1951** I wandered out into the night ... down a small, cobbled lane to where the Stour, sinister in the fading light, ebbed muddily to the distant sea.

All about me was the smell of half-tide mud-flats, it mingled with the smell of fresh-caught herrings sizzling in pans in the kitchens of near-by cottages - tiny dwellings whose windows glowed like the eyes of well-fed cats across the marshes where once the sea had flowed.

I went back along Strand Street, past the old grey tower of the church. ... I gazed out ... at the orange-green sky, streaked with gonfalons of brilliant red, harbingers of wind of the morrow.

Then night shut down on the ancient and forgotten port of Sandwich like the black shadow of the wings of Hugin (G. Carter).[96]

**1976** A bypass is planned for the town, which will sweep round to the west of it. This will reduce the money got from tolls but will save the little town from absolute destruction by traffic. ... Yachts can get up to Sandwich, and the toll bridge will lift to let them go even farther up. At the quay there is ten foot of water at spring's high water and a dubious six and a half foot at neaps. If you go through the bridge there are twelve miles of river with four foot of water, and with twelve foot briggage ... under the railway. Smafl boats can get to Fordwich, fifteen miles up ... As to what there is to see nowadays in Sandwich, it is a very lovely little town, with a mixture of medieval, Tudor and Georgian buildings in it. ... The Barbican, by the Toll Bridge, is of the time of Henry VIII, the Fisher Gate, east of this, 1384, and one can walk round the town, almost, on the earth ramparts. There are some fine private houses, Manwood Court is a Dutch-looking brick building, very fine, with the date 1564 on it ... St. Bartholomew's Hospital, just off the Dover Road, was founded in 1190 as a hostel for travellers. It has a thirteenth century chapel. The King's House, near St. Mary's Church, has fifteenth century timber framing hidden by eighteenth century brick, St. Clement's Church has one of the finest Norman towers in Kent, and the cottage in which Tom Paine lived ... is in New Street.

When the bypass has been achieved, and the absolute <u>persecution</u> by traffic has ceased in the narrow streets, Sandwich will be an enchanting little place to be (J. Seymour).[97]

**References and Bibliography.**

1. Schassek, "The journey of a Bohemian Ambassador to Canterbury" in A.P. Stanley, *Historical Memorials of Canterbury*. (1904). G. Gray, *Sandwich, the Story of a Famous Kentish Port*. (1907).

2. J. Gairdner (Ed.), *A Short English Chronicle*. (The Camden Society). (1870).

3. H. Ellis, *The New Chronicles of England and France in Two Parts by Robert Fabyan*. (1811).

4. *Letters and Papers; Foreign and Domestic of the Reign of Henry VIII, III, Part 1*, Letter from Bishop of Elna and Jehan de la Sauch to the Emperor Charles V. (1867).

5. *Calendar of Letters, Despatches and State Papers Relating to the Negotiations between England and Spain II. Henry VIII, 1509-1525*. (1866).

6. L. Toulmin Smith, *The Itinerary of John Leland in or About the Years 1535-1543*. (1964).

7. H. Ellis, *The New Chronicles of England and France in Two Parts by Robert Fabyan*. (1811).

8. J. Strype, *The Life and Acts of Matthew Parker*. (1821). I. Book II.

9. W. Lambarde. *A Perambulation of* Kent. (1570).

10. W. Boys, *Collections for an History of Sandwich in Kent*. (1792).

11. G.T. Copley (Ed.), *Camden's Britannia. Kent*. (1977).

12. G.B. Harrison, *The Elizabethan Journals: Being a Record of Those Things Most Talked of During the Years 1591-1603. The last Elizabethan Journal, 1599-1603*. (1955).

13. *The Journal of William Schellinks' Travels in England, 1661-1663*, Camden Fifth Series, I. Royal Historical Society. (1993).

14. L.G. Wickham Legg (Ed.), *A relation of a short survey of the Western Counties made by a Lieutenant of the Military Company in Norwich on 1635*. (Camden Miscellany.) XVI. (1936).

15. E.S. De Beer (Ed.), *The Diary of John Evelyn*. (1959).

16. Thomas Baskerville, *An Account of Some Remarkable Things in a Journey Between London and Dover*. Historical Manuscripts Commission, Thirteenth Report, Appendix Part II. (1893).

17. W. Somner, *The History of the Roman Ports and Forts in Kent*. (1693).

18. C. Morris (Ed.), *The Journey of Celia Fiennes*. (1949).

19. J. Harris, *The History of Kent in Five Parts.* (1719).

20. J. Lewis, *The History and Antiquities of the Isle of Tenet in Kent.* (1723).

21. D. Defoe, *A Tour Through the Whole Island of Great Britain.* (1724).

22. W. Boys, *Collections for An History of Sandwich in Kent.* (1792).

23. J.J. Cartwright (Ed.), *The Travels Through England of Dr. Richard Pocock.* (The Camden Society.) II. (1889).

24. M. Pennington, *Memoirs of the Life of Mrs. Elizabeth Carter.* (1807).

25. *The Journal of the Rev. John Wesley.* (1895).

26. T. Philipott, *Villare Cantianum; or Kent Surveyed and Illustrated.* (1776).

27. Lady Mary Coke (*Letter from Margate*). (1783).

28. Lady Mary Coke (*Letter from Ramsgate*). (1788).

29. *The Journal of the Rev. John Wesley.* (1895).

30. W. Boys, *Collections for An History of Sandwich in Kent.* (1792).

31. A. Young, 'Some Farming Notes in Essex, Kent and Sussex', *Annals of Agriculture.* XX. (1793).

32. T. Fisher, *The Kentish Traveller's Companion.* (1794).

33. J. Boys, *General View of the Agriculture of the County of Kent.* (1794).

34. E. Hasted, *The History and Topographical Survey of the County of Kent.* (1800).

35. T. Lot, *A Journey to Dover, Deal and Canterbury.* (1815).

36. J. Fussell, *A Journey round the Coast of Kent.* (1818).

37. E.W. Brayley, *Delineations Historical and Topographical of the Isle of Thanet and the Cinque Ports.* (1818).

38. T.K. Cromwell, *Excursions in the County of Kent.* (1822).

39. W. Cobbett, *Rural Rides.* (1830).

40. F. Hull (Ed.), "A Kentish Holiday, 1823", in M. Roake and J. Whyman, *Essays in Kentish History.* (1973).

41. W.A. Pettman, *A Brief Statement of the Benefits and Advantages to be Derived from Opening a Communication by the River Stour Between Canterbury and Sandwich.* (1824).

42. *Pigot and Co.'s Commercial Directory.* (1824).

43. Boundary Commissioners, *Report on the Town and Port of Sandwich*, PP. HoC, XXXIX. (1831-2).

44. *Pigot and Co.'s Commercial Directory*. (1832-34).

45. *Reports from His Majesty's Commissioners for Inquiring into the Administration and Practical Operation of the Poor Laws. Appendix (A). Reports of Assistant Commissioners*. Part I. PP. HoC. XXVIII. (1834).

46. *Appendix (Part II) to the First Report of the Commissioners of the Municipal Corporations of England and Wales, South-Eastern and Southern Circuits. The Town of Sandwich.* PP. HoC. XXIV, 3. (1835).

47. *Kent Herald*, 13 July, 1837.

48. C. Greenwood, *An Epitome of County History: I - The County of Kent*. (1838).

49. *The Watering Places of Great Britain and Fashionable Directory*. (1838).

50. A. Twyman, *In Search of the Mysterious Doctor Weekes (A fragment of Sandwich History)*. (1988).

51. *The Post Office Directory*. (1845).

52. S. Bagshaw, *History, Gazetteer and Directory of the County of Kent*. (1847).

53. *The Visitors' New Guide (Historical and Descriptive) to the Isle of Thanet*. (1850).

54. G. Measom, *Official Illustrated Guide to the South Eastern Railway*. (1858).

55. Mackenzie Walcott, *A Guide to the South Coast of England*. (1859).

56. *Kelly's Directory of Kent*. (1859).

57. J. Murray, *A Handbook for Travellers in Kent and Sussex*. (1863).

58. R. Jenkins, "The History of Sandwich", in *Archaeologia Cantiana*, VI. (1866).

59. W. Miller, *Jottings of Kent*. (1871).

60. D. Gardiner, *Historic Haven. The story of Sandwich*. (1954).

61. A. and C. Black, *Black's Guide to Kent*. (1874).

62. S. Smiles, *The Huguenots, Their Settlement, Churches and Industries in England and Ireland*. (1876).

63. *Report of the Commissioners Appointed ... to Inquire into the Existence of Corrupt Practices in the Borough of Sandwich. II: Minutes of Evidence*. PP. HoC, XLV. (1881)

64. *Report of the Commissioners Appointed ... to Inquire into the Existence of Corrupt Practices in the Borough of Sandwich. II. Minutes of Evidence.* PP. HoC, XLV. (1881).

65. G. Phillips Bevan, *Handbook to the County of Kent.* (1887).

66. M. Burrows, *Cinque Ports.* (1888).

67. W. Clark Russell, *Betwixt the Forelands.* (1889).

68. G.B. Griffin, *Sandwich: A Descriptive and Historical Sketch.* (1890).

69. J. Hatton, *The Old House at Sandwich.* (1894).

70. F.C. Burnand, *The ZZG or Zig Zag Guide Round and About the Bold and Beautiful Kentish Coast.* (1897).

71. J.L.F.H.M. Hueffer, *The Cinque Ports. A Historical and Descriptive Record.* (1900).

72. D. Moul and G. Thompson, *Picturesque Kent. A Historical and Descriptive Record.* (1901).

73. W.W. Jacobs, *At Sunwich Port.* (1902).

74. W. Dexter, "A Day in the Isle of Thanet", *The Boys' Own Paper.* XXV. (1903).

75. *Deal, Walmer and Sandwich Illustrated.* (c. 1904).

76. E. Walford, *Pleasant Days in Pleasant Places.* (1905).

77. C.G. Harper, *The Ingoldsby Country.* (1906).

78. W. Jerrold, *Highways and Byways in Kent.* (1907).

79. G. Gray, *Sandwich: The Story of a Famous Kentish Port.* (1907).

80. *Kelly's Directory of Kent.* (1907).

81. W.T. Shore, *Kent.* (1907).

82. *Pike's Deal, Walmer and Sandwich Blue Book and Local Directory.* (1910).

83. W.G. Gordon, *Sandwich and Round About It.* (1910).

84. J.L. Roget, *Sketches of Deal, Walmer and Sandwich.* (1911).

85. A.D. Lewis, *The Kent Coast.* (1911).

86. P. Row (Ed.), *Southern England Coast and Countryside.* (1913).

87. C.G. Harper, *The Kentish Coast.* (1914).

88. F. Watt, *Canterbury Pilgrims and their Ways.* (1917).

89. A.G. Bradley, *England's Outpost. The Country of the Kentish Cinque Ports.* (1921).
90. *The Cornhill Magazine.* (1924).
91. P. Abercrombie, *East Kent Regional Planning Scheme: Preliminary Scheme.* (1925).
92. C. Igglesden, *A Saunter Through Kent with Pen and Pencil.* (1926).
93. A. Mee, *The King's England: Kent.* (1936).
94. R. Wyndham, *South-Eastern Survey: A Last Look Round Sussex, Kent and Surrey.* (1940).
95. S.P.B. Mais, *The Land of the Cinque Ports.* (1946).
96. G. Goldsmith Carter, *Forgotten Ports of England.* (1951).
97. J. Seymour, *The Companion Guide to The Coast of South-East England.* (1976).